MAKING QUALITY WORK

MAKING
QUALITY
WORK

A LEADERSHIP GUIDE FOR THE
RESULTS-DRIVEN MANAGER

GEORGE LABOVITZ,
YU SANG CHANG,
VICTOR ROSANSKY

omneo

An imprint of Oliver Wight Publications, Inc.
85 Allen Martin Drive
Essex Junction, VT 05452

CONTENTS

Acknowledgments   vii

Introduction   1

1 ▪ Road Map to World-Class   11

2 ▪ The Trade-off Trap   21

3 ▪ What Once Came Naturally . . .   29

4 ▪ Quality: "The Unfair Advantage"   47

5 ▪ From Caveat Emptor to Customer-Supplier Partnership   69

6 ▪ The Magic Ingredient   91

7 ▪ Leading Customer-Focused Breakthrough   109

8 ▪ Changing Your World   147

APPENDICES

Appendix A: Rating Your TQM Implementation   159

Appendix B: The Deming Prize and the Baldrige Award   167

Appendix C: The Pillars of Quality   175

Appendix D: "FADE"   177

Appendix E: Selected Articles   179

Appendix F: Suggested Readings   191

Appendix G: About Organizational Dynamics, Inc.   193

Index   194

INTRODUCTION

WHAT IS TOTAL QUALITY MANAGEMENT?

Total quality management (TQM) is a relatively new approach to the art of management. It seeks to improve product and service quality and increase customer satisfaction by restructuring traditional management practices. The application of TQM is unique to each organization that adopts such an approach.

—REPORT OF THE U.S. GENERAL ACCOUNTING OFFICE,
May 1991

It seems that what you're telling us boils down to five basic principles:

1) Ask customers what they want.
2) Set zero defects as your standard.
3) Complete work in the shortest possible time.
4) Measure the system, not personal behavior.
5) Make sure everyone feels like a stakeholder.

—U.S. CONGRESSMAN NEWT GINGRICH,
responding to testimony about total quality management

In the summer of 1990, we experienced one of those moments when an elusive truth at last comes clear. We had just led a group of U.S. executives through Japan's Kansai Electric Company—winner of the prestigious Deming Prize for quality strategy, management, and execution—and were exchanging pleasantries with our hosts.

"Some IBM executives were here on a study visit just yesterday," one Kansai executive noted. "They told us that, at IBM, total quality management is seventy percent attitude and only thirty percent quality control technique." He then frowned and silently shook his head. We could guess what he was thinking. Such a "soft" approach to managing quality might be acceptable in the United States, but it would never pass muster in Japan.

We were wrong. "In Japan," the Kansai executive concluded, "total quality management is *ninety* percent attitude."

That revelation affirmed, in a sense, a journey that began some ten years before, in the fall of 1980, at the Boston University Faculty Club. Yu Sang ("Charlie") Chang, professor of operations management, had just returned from an extended stay in the Far East, where he had served as senior adviser to Byung Chull Lee, the late chairman of the mammoth Samsung Group. Once home, Chang sought out his colleague George Labovitz, professor of organizational behavior and management. Something very important and very exciting was happening in the Far East, Chang insisted. That "something" was "total quality control."

Labovitz listened courteously to his friend, but to him the term "quality control" conjured up dreary images of inspection reports, control charts, and white-jacketed men writing on clipboards. Sure, all that stuff was important. But quality control had little to do with what intrigued Labovitz about management.

Labovitz's interest was *people*. What motivates them? Why do they behave as they do? Most importantly, how can managers focus more of their employees' energy and abilities on *achieving objectives?* After all, Labovitz stressed in his lectures, managers aren't paid to make employees feel good. They are paid to get work done.

In fact, Labovitz had founded a consulting and training company to help managers grapple with just those kinds of issues. And the company was doing well. By 1980, scores of Fortune 500 companies and hundreds of hospitals nationwide were using management and supervisory training programs developed by Organiza-

ACKNOWLEDGMENTS

The acknowledgments appropriate for a book of this nature could easily run as long as the book itself (but we promise to restrain ourselves).

First, our colleague Tom Varian worked with us each step of the way to conceptualize, write, and edit this text. If not for his talents and perseverance, there would be no book at all.

Just over a year ago Robert Chapman Wood convinced us it was time to write *our* book on total quality management, and he was always there for us in times of need. His encouragement, input, and experience were invaluable.

The ideas presented in *Making Quality Work* are not all our own. Far from it. They are the harvest of a unique organization, Organizational Dynamics, Inc., of which the three of us are but a part. We gladly acknowledge our debt to our ODI colleagues and convey our genuine delight in belonging to that extraordinary band of brothers and sisters.

Finally, there are our customers—a collection of business, health care, government, and other organizations so diverse that it defies categorization, let alone acknowledgment, in the space available here. Yet the countless executives, managers, and employees whom we've served over the years all share at least two things in common: They are all dedicated to making quality work. And they have all taught us something.

GEORGE H. LABOVITZ
YU SANG CHANG
VICTOR I. ROSANSKY

MAKING QUALITY WORK

tional Dynamics, Inc. (ODI). Business was booming. There was no compelling reason for Labovitz to become a devotee of total quality control.

Still, Chang's report on what Japanese companies were achieving was too impressive to ignore. Labovitz decided to watch this new approach, just as he had studied Management by Objectives, Zero Defects, and any other management innovation that promised to make organizations more effective.

Then Florida Power & Light (FP&L) called. By 1981, Marshall McDonald, chairman of FP&L, had independently arrived at the same conclusion as Chang—total quality control was important— and he was determined to make his company an American show-case of total quality management. FP&L selected ODI to help develop new programs for its total quality training curriculum.

An ODI project team led by the third author, Victor Rosansky, was dispatched to Miami, where they set up housekeeping in a condo a few blocks from FP&L headquarters. The assignment, Rosansky soon learned, was to convert a nine-inch-thick binder of quality control concepts and techniques into training that would be palatable to FP&L's American managers and employees. Thus, ODI entered the quality management field.

Although our experience up to that point had been almost entirely in the traditional realm of management training and devel-opment, we realized that training alone could not make this thing called "total quality" come alive. Between the cup and the lip— between training people in quality improvement techniques and enabling them to actually *implement* a total quality approach in the workplace—something was missing. Managers and employees had needs that even the best quality training programs could not meet. However, we were still too new to the field to identify or articulate those needs.

We worked with FP&L managers and employees for several

years, learning a great deal from them about the basics of Japanese-style total quality control as we helped develop programs for their quality training curriculum. During this period Chang joined ODI, bringing with him years of research in total quality control and a vast network of expert contacts in the Far East. Chang also introduced his ODI colleagues to the teachings of W. Edwards Deming, Kaoru Ishikawa, Joseph Juran, and Armand Feigenbaum—the great masters of total quality.

By 1985, our work with FP&L was done. And ODI emerged from that fortuitous engagement into a business environment in which everyone, it seemed, was suddenly intrigued with total quality.

By the mid-1980s, many U.S. companies (especially in manufacturing) had instituted statistical process control (SPC) programs and had experimented with quality circles. But while the former provided useful data and the latter involved people in quality, neither approach was clearly connected to the other *or* to management's business priorities.

In contrast, "total" quality promised that the power of SPC, employee involvement, and team problem-solving systems could be effectively combined and focused on management's strategic goals. Gradually, a subtle but significant shift occurred in the U.S. vernacular. The term "total quality *control*" (or "total quality improvement") was superseded by "total quality *management*," a sign that quality had become a mainstream management issue.

There were, of course, less subtle clues. Philip Crosby's *Quality Is Free* (1979) became a bestseller among business books. In our view, Crosby's single greatest contribution (among many) was not proving that improving quality is cost effective. Rather, it was his success in convincing managers that quality is their issue. He talked about quality in language that truly moved business people—even those who did not share his technical background. *Quality Is Free* convinced many business leaders that quality is too vital a responsibility to delegate to a quality assurance or quality control function.

With quality now firmly entrenched as the "hot issue" in business, many consultants rushed to preach the gospel of total quality management (TQM). Others debated the finer points of total quality theory. But we at ODI focused on the implementation question: How could the core tenets and techniques of TQM be effectively *applied* in business organizations?

ODI's next major TQM engagement was with Procter & Gamble. P&G had recently put 9,000 of its people through statistical process control training and had sent 100 of its key managers to participate in Dr. Deming's week-long total quality seminar. But only 5 percent of P&G employees trained in SPC were actually using the tool in their jobs. And P&G managers, though convinced of the truth and importance of Dr. Deming's ideas, were struggling to put them into action. So far, TQM had taken hold only in pockets of the company.

One cause of the inertia at P&G, we soon learned, was that it was hard for a company with such a long and proud tradition to embrace new ways of doing things. P&G wasn't in trouble. It was a monumental success story with a winning streak dating back 150 years. Why change?

But Vice Chairman Tom Laco didn't buy that line of thinking. "P&G is a great company," he said, "and we're implementing total quality to *stay* great." In a sentence, Laco had removed all stigma from the idea that a winning company needs to improve quality. We've since seen Laco's reasoning confirmed in dozens of other proud, successful client organizations.

Still, telling people that total quality management is necessary is not the same as convincing them to use TQM tools. A P&G engineer hit the nail right on the head when he told us, "These things you call quality tools are really concepts. They're just disguised as tools." He was right. And if people don't believe in the concepts, they won't use the tools.

Therefore, the main issue at P&G was culture change, not skills training. We've since found that the same can be said of every organization that has ever tried to implement total quality management.

P&G's Tom Laco also gave us an early clue to the power of one of the central concepts of this book: alignment. As you shall see, we contend that the business leader's most fundamental task is to align the organization's employees and work processes with ever-changing customer requirements.

The first time we diagrammed the alignment concept was with P&G executives in one of our early senior management briefings circa 1985. Alignment was just one of many topics on the agenda that day, so we did not dwell on it. The next day, however, Laco told us, "I didn't sleep very well last night. I was thinking about that alignment idea. It's crucial. You just didn't explain it very well."

Laco then proceeded to explain the strategic significance of alignment to *us* and spelled out in no uncertain terms how central the alignment concept is for any company seeking competitive advantage in the marketplace. Needless to say, since then we've never made short shrift of alignment when talking to senior managers.

In 1987, Federal Express became one of our largest and most significant clients in that our work there has provided some of our most meaningful learning experiences. For example, our precept that world-class leaders must learn to hear and balance three "voices"—The Voice of the Customer, The Voice of the Employee, and The Voice of the Process—was formed in large part from observing the leaders of Federal Express (especially Fred Smith, chairman and CEO).

Federal Express also convinced us that management really can use quality measurement systems to drive large corporations toward strategic objectives . . . *if* the measures are relatively simple and *if* the measures have consequences. Federal Express data-gathering mechanisms, such as the Service Quality Indicator and Survey-Feedback-Action (both of which are described in these pages), boil down input from thousands of data points into a few key numbers. Everyone—senior managers, middle managers, and employees— uses these highly visible scorecards to gauge his or her collective and individual performance.

In 1988 (three years after Tom Laco enlightened us on the strategic significance of alignment), Procter & Gamble furnished us with yet another invaluable learning opportunity. The consumer products giant asked Victor Rosansky to facilitate a customer-supplier work conference for its senior managers and the senior management team of Wal-Mart. That unique episode (starring the one-and-only Sam Walton) is detailed in Chapter Five. For now, we'll simply note that the assignment gave us a glimpse into the future of total quality—into an era when companies will learn how to delight not just their own customers, but their *customers'* customers as well.

Which brings us to why we wrote this book. Of the thousands of TQM publications already in print, we know of none that truly explains how to wield quality as a competitive weapon. Yet, in the world of business, competition is what makes quality important. A TQM effort that "involves people" but fails to enhance your competitive advantage is *not* functional, no matter how good it makes you and your employees feel.

The last thing the world needs then is another book about "committing to quality." Today, business leaders want practical input on "making quality work." They want to know how they can *use* TQM to significantly increase their customers' (and potential customers') desire to do business with their organization. That is what this book is all about.

We believe that the key to making quality work is *leadership*, as indicated in the subtitle of this text: "A Leadership Guide for the Results-Driven Manager." Although at times we will speak of leadership in the abstract, for the most part we will advocate a particular kind of leadership, which we have labeled "world-class" leadership.

Today, of course, business competition is conducted on a global scale. No market, product, or service is impervious to competition. And your next competitor may emerge from any spot on the globe. World-class leadership, then, can be defined as leadership that prepares the organization to withstand any competitive threat, from any source.

The tools of world-class leadership are still TQM tools. The difference is mostly one of perspective. World-class leaders don't fixate on one or two aspects of TQM (e.g., zero defects or customer satisfaction). They see the big picture of quality. What's more, they make certain that every manager and employee in their company sees the big picture, too. And that's not easy. As Fred Smith says, when it comes to improving quality, "The hard stuff is easy. It's the soft stuff that's hard."

By "soft stuff" Smith means clear communication of values and priorities, inspirational vision, leading by example, and enhancing customer-supplier relationships. People need these things to excel for their customers.

Of course, they also need "hard" skills, such as those that Chang first saw applied to such powerful effect in the Far East. But lack of skills does not appear to be the main obstacle to quality improvement. Countless thousands of employees have been trained in TQM. The problem is, this training is rarely accompanied by the clear, consistent, compelling *leadership* employees need to apply their skills to full effect.

For most managers, the conceptual distance between "hard" quality improvement skills and "softer" notions of quality leadership has seemed too great to bridge, just as the conceptual distance between Chang, the professor of operations management, and Labovitz, the professor of organizational behavior, once seemed to preclude our effective collaboration.

Yet this distance must be bridged. For until managers learn how to provide both practical quality skills and inspirational quality leadership to their people, they are destined to fall short of their quality and customer satisfaction objectives.

World-class leaders work *for* their people. They keep them attuned to rapidly changing conditions and help them gain extraordinary insights into customer needs and preferences. They give employees the skills, knowledge, and power required to effect change. And they inspire their people to reach beyond basic customer requirements, to provide the uncommon, unexpected dimensions of quality and service that delight, rather than merely satisfy, their customers. This, above all else, is the message we wish to share with you. When you can provide value even your customers hadn't anticipated, you are wielding quality as a competitive weapon. You are making quality work.

We arrived at these conclusions through direct observation. Today, ODI is an international consulting firm with more than two hundred professionals serving clients in North America, Europe, Central America, Asia, and Australia. We have had more opportunities than most to observe great business leaders in action.

The leaders we cite in these pages as examples of world-class leadership are not perfect. They are human. And the companies they lead remain subject to the ups and downs of market competition. But in an imperfect world, these leaders consistently exhibit abilities and behaviors that the reader would be wise to embrace. Their stories document a fundamental truth, one which we came to recognize over the course of a decade: Making quality work really is "ninety percent attitude"—*your* attitude.

1 ■ ROAD MAP TO WORLD-CLASS

DILBERT by Scott Adams

"I am sick and tired of visiting plants to hear nothing but great things about quality and cycle time only to then visit customers who tell me of problems."

The lament of a second-rate company? Hardly. The quote is from former IBM CEO John Akers, who voiced his frustration in a recent *Wall Street Journal* article.[1] We imagine that more than a few of the *Journal*'s 1.5 million readers sympathized with Akers's dilemma.

In fact, the business press has reported the failure of corporate efforts to improve quality in several stories. Over one six-month span we spotted such headlines as

- WHEN QUALITY CONTROL GETS IN THE WAY OF QUALITY (*Wall Street Journal*)
- THE CRACKS IN QUALITY (*The Economist*)
- QUALITY PROGRAMS SHOW SHODDY RESULTS (*Wall Street Journal*)
- WHAT'S WRONG WITH TOTAL QUALITY MANAGEMENT? (*Tapping the Network Journal*)

■ 11 ■

The Economist piece is particularly damning. "A staggering number of companies are discovering that quality street is a dead end," the article states. Then, citing research conducted by various management consulting firms, it adds ". . . of those quality programmes that have been in place in Western firms for more than two years, two-thirds simply grind to a halt because of their failure to produce the hoped-for results."[2]

Are the journalists who wrote these articles misguided fools? Hopelessly biased cynics? We don't think so. Some advocates of total quality management (TQM) have since issued forceful rebuttals (e.g., see "Shoddy Results or Shoddy Reporting?" *Quality Digest,* August 1992). But we acknowledge that more than a few organizations are legitimately disappointed in TQM. Somehow, despite million-dollar training budgets and quality team activity that resembles the inner workings of a beehive, these companies have yet to produce the visible, tangible results needed to satisfy the CEO.

What's more, we think we know why. And it is *not* because "quality street is a dead end." Rather, for many organizations TQM has become like a giant traffic circle. They find themselves going around and around, expending precious energy, searching in vain for a sign that tells them where to proceed next on their quality journey. These wayward travelers don't need doomsayers. They need a good road map—one that tells them where they have been, where they stand now, and where to go next.

YOUR STAGE OF TQM REVOLUTION

Most organizations follow a predictable path in their TQM evolution, which we describe in four stages: 1) Awakening, 2) Active, 3) Breakthrough, and 4) World-Class. As we review each stage, look for the characteristics that describe your organization. How far have you progressed on your quality journey? What lies ahead for you?

	Stage 1 Awakening	Stage 2 Active	Stage 3 Breakthrough	Stage 4 World-Class
	The Awakening organization....	The Active organization....	The Breakthrough organization....	The World-Class organization....
Achievement Orientation *What the organization tries to do*	Is focused on short-term financial results.	Senses need to shift focus to longer-term outcomes.	Seeks long-term customer relationships, even at the expense of short-term financial results.	Exists to delight customers.
Improvement Orientation *What the organization tries to improve*	Tries to exploit its greatest strengths.	Tries to identify and analyze its shortcomings.	Focuses on improving a critical few work processes.	Seeks to consistently "lead" customers by providing extraordinary, unanticipated value.
Data Orientation *What information the organization uses*	Relies almost exclusively on data generated from traditional, internal sources (i.e., budgets, revenue, and manufacturing/ operations costs).	Is fascinated with new sources of data.	Tries to link its internal process data with external customer data.	Continuously seeks stream of integrated data from the market environment, customers, employees, and work processes.
Functional Orientation *How the organization sees itself*	Is "turf" oriented.	Experiments with alternatives to "turfism." Attempts to cut across its functional chimneys with quality programs.	Systematically fights "turfism." Seeks to achieve cross-functional focus on shared, customer-defined goals.	Has eliminated "turfism." All functions share same goal: Delight customers.
Catalytic Orientation *What causes the organization to change*	Responds to crisis.	Seeks to escape crisis mode with new emphasis on prevention.	Responds to what it thinks customers want.	Responds to opportunity.
Emotional Orientation *How people in the organization feel*	Is staffed by frustrated or indifferent employees.	Is staffed by skeptical employees.	Is staffed by motivated, spirited employees.	Is staffed by confident, empowered employees.

STAGE 1: AWAKENING

In Stage 1, management is just "awakening" to the need for change. Suddenly, there is much talk about quality and the importance of satisfying customers. Managers start to question some of their long-standing assumptions about what they must do to secure the organization's future. Complacency gives way to an ill-defined sense that "we have to do something."

Still, the Awakening organization has not yet changed in any concrete sense. Nor is it systematically pursuing change. Instead, management still tries to exploit whatever it perceives to be the organization's greatest *current* strengths in the hope of maximizing short-term financial results.

In keeping with their limited aspirations, managers in the Awakening organization demand and use very limited data in guiding the company. This data is primarily derived from internal sources, and it suggests a highly reactive mindset. It offers management only a narrow picture of the recent past and foretells almost nothing of the future.

The various functions within the organization operate with relative autonomy, mainly because turf issues block effective cross-functional communication and cooperation. Decisions are made at the top and handed down through a vertical management hierarchy. Each function therefore pursues an agenda that is only marginally connected with the agendas of the other functions.

The Awakening organization is slow to respond to changing conditions, often standing still until confronted with a crisis. It then expends a great deal of energy, time, and resources trying to fix or make good on problems. The causes of these problems are generally unknown, in large part because customer contact is limited and customer input is sporadic, coming mostly in the form of complaints or bid specifications.

Finally, the employees of the Awakening organization recognize that they have no real voice in important decisions and that they lack meaningful opportunities to "make a difference." Nor do they share in management's principal Achievement orientation, as they have no immediate stake in the company's short-term financial gains. At this stage, employees often feel frustrated, resentful, or (at best) emotionally uninvolved. They maintain a healthy detachment from a work environment that neither challenges nor rewards them.

STAGE 2: ACTIVE

The changes that take place as the organization moves from the Awakening to the Active stage can be dazzling, at least on the surface. The Active organization's senior managers have "got religion" about quality. With their eyes now opened to the vast potential for improvement within their organization, they unleash a torrent of activity designed to resolve its quality problems (usually termed "opportunities for improvement").

Stage 2 is often marked, for example, by large-scale quality training efforts and the rapid proliferation of employee quality teams. However, this activity is not highly coordinated, is not yet targeted to clear priorities, and is not easily measured in terms of added value to the company.

Still, important progress is being made. The Active organization is building an essential base of quality awareness and quality improvement skills. Its managers recognize that their focus on short-term financial results is inadequate and they consciously expand their goals to include more long-term and more customer-focused outcomes. Further, their improvement orientation shifts from trying to leverage the organization's current strengths toward understanding and addressing its most significant weaknesses.

The Active organization is fascinated with new sources of data. Its leaders often visit other companies to learn how to augment their own meager information resources. In most cases, this is also the point at which the organization first attempts to systematically gather data from its customers, employees, and work processes through surveys, fundamental statistical process control, and other formal and ongoing methods.

Turf is still a significant issue in the Active organization, but it makes its first attempts to break through its functional "chimneys" by raising awareness of "the importance of the customer," forming a few cross-functional teams, articulating organization-wide quality improvement themes, etc. At this stage, many organizations also initiate suggestion systems, start to conduct open forums for exchanges between employees and senior management, and pursue other activities designed to stimulate "bottom up" communication.

By Stage 2, the organization's leaders are painfully aware of the high costs of operating in a crisis mode. Of course, this alone does not put an end to crises. But it does lead to a new emphasis on *prevention* of quality problems and to a closer examination of the causes of crises. This in turn initiates the long and vital process of change required to escape the "firefighting" mind-set prevalent in most companies.

Employees of the Active organization are skeptical. They hear their managers espousing unfamiliar beliefs and behaving in new ways, and they can't help but wonder how long it will all last. Most employees enter quality training and participate in early quality improvement activities not because they are inspired to do so, but because it is what management requires. Some grouse about the "extra work" TQM requires of them. Fortunately, employees' skepticism gradually fades as they realize "TQM is here to stay." Commitment to the organization tends to grow in tandem with increasing opportunities for employees to initiate change and participate in decision making.

Active organizations typically make significant and valuable gains in eliminating waste and rework. However, these gains often pale in comparison to what senior management believes the organization *could* and *should* achieve through TQM.

STAGE 3: BREAKTHROUGH

The operative word to describe Stage 3 is focus. The Breakthrough organization above all else seeks to establish long-term customer relationships. It tries to form joint strategies and agendas with its key customers, then focuses its process improvement capabilities on improving work processes that are most critical to generating whatever customers say would constitute exceptional added value.

The Breakthrough organization prizes any data that suggest opportunities for quantum leaps in customer satisfaction and customer loyalty. It constantly compares data on its internal operations against data and input about (and from) customers, searching for gaps between customer expectations and its own capabilities.

Because the organization now fully recognizes that "turfism" hinders efforts to meet customer expectations, it systematically attacks all vestiges of turf-based behavior. Titular heads of functions learn that their individual agendas must take a back seat to the organization-wide focus on meeting or exceeding customer requirements.

By now, the organization rarely operates in crisis mode and is therefore increasingly free to explore how it might exceed customer expectations. The Breakthrough organization *seeks* change, because it recognizes that only through change can it draw its customers into long-term relationships.

Employees of the Breakthrough organization are motivated by what they perceive as real opportunities to positively affect customer satisfaction. And they are anxious to focus their analytical and quality problem-solving skills on objectives that are clearly important to their managers and to successful business.

STAGE 4: WORLD-CLASS

As defined here, World-Class is an idealized state. No organization exhibits all these characteristics all of the time. But we think it is important to contrast this ideal state with the actual state in which most organizations reside.

The World-Class organization exists to delight customers, confident that it will achieve long-term growth and exceptional profitability. Rather than simply repeating what worked best for them in the past, its world-class leaders constantly redefine the organization's strengths and weaknesses, modifying their improvement objectives in step with new (and even anticipated) customer needs and expectations.

The World-Class organization is continuously bathed in a stream of integrated data describing the interplay of its market environment, customers, employees, and work processes. By Stage 4, "turfism" is dead. The vertical or functional differentiations that defined the Awakening organization's self-image are now insignificant. What matters now is how work moves *horizontally* through the organization across its various functions, and how effectively all parts of the organization work together to delight customers.

Freed from the grip of crises, the World-Class organization is ever alert to new opportunities, which employees feel fully empowered to pursue.

CONCLUSION

How far has your organization advanced on its TQM journey? What must you do to progress to the next stage? You should ponder these questions frequently to maintain a clear sense of purpose and direction in your TQM process.

In fact, we believe that many of the organizations said to be hitting "a dead end on quality street" have in reality lost their sense of TQM direction at the end of Stage 2. Three to six years into their

TQM implementations, these organizations have developed (at significant cost and through great effort) a formidable TQM capability. They have trained their employees in quality principles and prepared them to apply proven quality improvement skills in their jobs. The problem is their leaders are not sure just what to *do* with this TQM capability. Perhaps it is because since they have focused so long on mastering the means of TQM, they've lost sight of its ends. Whatever the reason, they are clearly struggling to use TQM to build competitive advantage. It was for this group more than any other that we wrote *Making Quality Work*.

Even if you have just begun your quality journey, we have much to share with you. We will help you avoid the traps that often ensnare quality leaders. And we will explain just what you must do to

1) identify quality improvement objectives that are truly vital to the success of your organization,

2) focus your organization's TQM capability on achieving these objectives, and

3) dramatically accelerate your advance toward world-class performance.

To begin, let us next offer a fresh perspective on your most fundamental leadership responsibility—decision making.

NOTES

1. Graham Sharman, "When Quality Control Gets in the Way of Quality," *Wall Street Journal*, February 24, 1992.

2. "The Cracks in Quality," *The Economist*, April 18, 1992.

2. ■ THE TRADE-OFF TRAP

If you're like most managers, you are proud of your ability to make the "hard choices" required to run a successful business. But many times, managers who *think* they're making difficult but necessary choices are actually stepping blindly into a trap—The Trade-off Trap.

The Trade-off Trap limits you to hard choices—profitability *or* customer satisfaction, operating efficiency *or* employee morale, short-term gains *or* long-term viability—when in fact you don't have to make trade-offs at all.

World-class leaders consistently recognize and elude The Trade-off Trap. They know that customer loyalty, employee commitment, and operating efficiency are all essential elements of business success. Therefore, they refuse to trade off one for the other. Instead, they constantly endeavor to put *all* these base elements of competitive advantage to work for them at the same time.

If this sounds simple, we assure you that it is not. Most managers are thoroughly conditioned toward a trade-off mentality. For generations our business schools and great corporations have taught developing business leaders that management is "the Art and Science of Making Trade-offs." It should surprise no one that most managers habitually confront decisions in cost-benefit terms: "What must I give up to get what we need?" "Is the return likely to justify the sacrifice?"

To break free of The Trade-off Trap, you must first learn to view yourself and your organization in dramatically new terms. You must come to grips with the complex interplay of people, systems, and goals that determine your organization's success. And you must be prepared to "step out of the box" that now confines your leadership perspective to familiar ways of making decisions and guiding the work of others.

THREE VOICES

World-class leaders are extraordinarily sensitized to their environment. And the environment within business organizations can be described in terms of three "voices": The Voice of the Customer, The Voice of the Employee, and The Voice of the Process.

The Voice of the Customer

Business organizations exist to meet the needs of customers. Therefore, The Voice of the Customer guides world-class leaders' every action and decision. Their employees are also guided by The Voice of the Customer—literally in the case of employees who interact directly with customers and figuratively in the case of all other employees. World-class leaders make sure that everyone shares an accurate and actionable understanding of what customers need and value.

The Voice of the Employee

In manufacturing and service companies alike, employees are the primary instrument by which business leaders meet customer needs. Of course, employees are not "instruments" at all. They are *people*, the most complex beings on earth, and therefore the single most volatile determinant of business success. World-class leaders constantly seek out The Voice of the Employee—the sum total of what employees think, feel, need, and believe.

The Voice of the Process

Golfers who ignore the mechanics of their swing and note only how far the ball has traveled are routinely confounded by their inability to predict or control the outcome of their efforts. The same can be said of business leaders who care only about results. That is why world-class leaders continually tap into The Voice of the Process—data that tell them how work actually gets done in their organizations. By focusing on process data, world-class leaders are prepared to make effective, continuous adjustments to key work processes, thereby controlling and improving results.

INCOMPATIBLE DEMANDS

Is simply "hearing" these Voices what sets world-class leaders apart from other managers? No. Although we do find that world-class leaders tend to have more (and more useful) data at their command, *all* managers spend much of their professional lives trying to reconcile the seemingly incompatible demands of The Voice of the Customer, The Voice of the Employee, and The Voice of the Process.

For example, when an advertising agency's pitch for a major new campaign falls behind schedule, Anne, a typical account supervisor, assures her boss that she'll "pull out all the stops" to get it done. She initiates rush procedures and tells the designers, copywriters, media planners, and traffic managers on her account team that, once again, it's time to "burn the midnight oil."

The next five days are a blur of black coffee, team meetings, half-eaten deli sandwiches, grinding teeth, phone calls from angry spouses, and weary coworkers asking one another, "What the hell time *is* it, anyway?" Happily, this ordeal generates several first-rate creative concepts, plus a media buying strategy that could save the client more than a million dollars in the next year.

When the big day arrives, Anne is still on her feet, but barely. The flaming red tributaries in her eyes have been doused with Visine. The stress lines in her forehead are obscured by pancake makeup. She draws a deep breath, steadies her queasy stomach, and delivers the pitch.

The client loves it! There are handshakes all around, and the agency's principals find more than one opportunity to plant solid pats on Anne's back. Having scaled the highest mountain, she tucks her portfolio case and handbag under her arm and limps victoriously off into the west, where she will spend the next fourteen hours sleeping dreamlessly in her suburban home.

Is Anne "a good leader"? In the traditional scheme of things, she's not only a good leader, she's a hero. She kept her head. Rallied her troops. And did whatever *had* to be done to satisfy the customer.

But at what cost? Rush procedures are expensive. To meet the customer's expectations, Anne commandeered two additional graphic artists and an extra copywriter. She also called in a free-lance media planner at the eleventh hour (her regular guy was so tired, he kept getting the numbers wrong).

Of course, the agency won the business, so these short-term dollar outlays probably didn't hurt much. Too bad the same can't be said of the disruption to normal work processes.

To meet the proposal deadline, Anne took every member of her team (plus a few outside players) off line and put all their other work on hold. The following week, Anne and her agency will have to make up that lost ground, which means they'll be forced to make further departures from their ideal work processes, juggle more schedules, make more sacrifices in efficiency, and assume increased risks of quality problems.

Speaking of quality problems, the client will phone Anne in a few days to ask why the numbers in the written proposal don't add up. She will look into it and learn that, during the chaotic final hours of preparation, she forgot to brief the freelance media planner on the special discounts the agency had arranged. He therefore went ahead and "corrected" the numbers in the written plan by inserting standard media rates. "I thought that was what you brought me in to do," he'll explain to Anne. "I guess it was," she'll be forced to acknowledge.

Nor should we overlook the impact of Anne's decisions on her employees. True, they might take satisfaction in meeting the crunch deadline and pleasing the customer. But there is no mistaking the messages Anne has sent them: "Operations are not entirely under control." "The people in charge don't have their acts together." The next time Anne announces a schedule and explains how and when the work will be completed, no one could blame her people for wondering if she really knows what she's talking about.

While Anne initially succeeded in terms of hearing and responding to The Voice of the Customer, she lost significant ground in terms of The Voice of the Employee and The Voice of the Process. She made *trade-offs* to meet her deadline, and the price she is likely to pay includes falling behind schedule on other projects, lost credibility with her employees, and more embarrassing quality problems. Anne has laid a trap into which she herself will step.

UNORTHODOX APPROACHES

What might Anne do to reduce the harmful effects of future crises on her organization, her people, and herself?

She could seek a much closer planning partnership with her

clients, who did not appear in our hypothetical case until the day of the presentation. It may take time for them to get used to this unorthodox approach. But if Anne succeeds in involving her customers in the development of her proposals, she can tap into "early warning signals" that will lessen both the severity and frequency of customer-generated crises.

Anne could also involve her people in analyzing and improving the work processes by which they meet customer needs. She could actively solicit and cultivate their ideas for eliminating errors and rework (which are costly under any circumstances, but doubly so in times of crises). And she could seek opportunities to reduce the "cycle time" required to complete work, so the next time a rush situation arises, fewer resources will have to be diverted from other important tasks.

Of course none of these things will happen until Anne's readiness to meet the crisis of the moment is matched with a comparable dedication to finding better ways to get work done. She must focus not just on meeting deadlines, but also on becoming a partner to her customers, a lightning rod for employee input, and a champion of process improvement.

Clearly, all managers and their businesses would be better off if they could meet customer needs without compromising their standing with employees or sacrificing the efficiency of work processes. Why then don't all business leaders emulate world-class leaders and refuse to make trade-offs?

As previously mentioned, managers are routinely and explicitly conditioned to make decisions in a trade-off context. No one has fully stated the case for another approach.

Most managers (like Anne) find it's difficult enough to meet their customers' immediate demands. They do what is expedient, and understandably question anyone who implies they may be able to do more.

There are no shortcuts. Mastering the required skills and gaining the necessary insight and perspective required to escape The Trade-off Trap takes time and effort, as even the "self-made" world-class leaders we cite in this book would surely tell you.

Escaping The Trade-off Trap requires managers to adopt leadership approaches that will seem unusual in many business organizations. It takes courage to pursue new ideals, especially if your boss (or your boss's boss) hasn't bought into them. Most managers won't even try new approaches until the organizational culture explicitly supports a new direction.

And most significantly, few managers even recognize that there *is* a trade-off trap. By focusing solely on the positive short-term results generated by their actions, they fail to grasp that, in reality, they routinely deny their organization any chance for improved performance over the long term.

CONCLUSION

Many attributes and abilities distinguish world-class leaders, but none is more basic than their ability to recognize and escape The Trade-off Trap. World-class leaders don't necessarily try harder than typical managers—they just play by a different set of rules. Once they gain the experience and master the skills required to excel under these rules, they can dramatically reduce costs while literally delighting their customers. They can achieve quantum leaps in productivity while invigorating and inspiring the people who work for them. And they can rise to any competitive challenge, from any source, any place on the globe. In the next chapter, we will see that the road to world-class leadership takes you first to a surprising destination—your entrepreneurial roots.

3 ■ WHAT ONCE CAME NATURALLY . . .

DILBERT by Scott Adams

DILBERT reprinted by permission of UFS, INC.

Late in 1990, executives at Hewlett-Packard's Medical Products Division summoned Yu Sang Chang to their corporate headquarters in Wilmington, Massachusetts. The Hewlett-Packard execs were puzzled by the success of certain Far Eastern competitors and hoped Chang might shed some light on the subject.

Chang, speaking with the executives in a small conference room, described the senior executive diagnosis conducted within many Japanese firms, including some of those which competed with Hewlett-Packard. His main point was that Japanese executives and U.S. executives pose very different questions to their employees.

"Top executives at Toyota and NEC don't ask 'What's your variance from the sales forecast?' or 'How are you doing on budget?'," Chang explained. "Instead, they demand to know 'What can we do to help you serve your customers better?', 'How are your processes working?', and 'What's getting in your way?'"

Executives at the best Japanese companies act like "roaming ambassadors from the customer," Chang continued. They probe every part of the company to see if it is working as it should to meet customer needs and expectations. And while they can be ruthless in eliminating factors that work against customer satisfaction, they basically treat the people who work for them like customers themselves. "Japanese executives put themselves at middle managers' and employees' disposal, because these are the people with the power to actually resolve problems for the external customer," Chang said.

One of the Hewlett-Packard executives interrupted. "Hey," he said, "that sounds exactly like Bill Hewlett. You call this 'senior executive diagnosis' a Japanese approach," the executive noted, "but in the old days, Bill used to go around asking just those kinds of questions. He did the exact same thing."

THE VOICE OF THE CUSTOMER

It was a telling comment. We've heard similar reactions in more than a dozen companies. When we talk about The Voice of the Customer, about how customer needs and preferences must drive everything a company does, we often strike a primal chord, one that causes people to reminisce about simpler (albeit, less secure) times when their great companies were still defining the values and shaping the corporate character that would make them great.

People like to harken back to days when they felt thrillingly close to their customers. Sometimes drawing on personal experience, more often relying on company lore, they remember when losing one key account could mean shutting the doors forever, while gaining the customer's favor meant the lights would burn for at least one more month. Old timers and rookies alike look back on those uncertain times with unbridled fondness. Why?

Part of the answer is the universal tendency to view the past through rose-colored glasses. But there is more to it than that.

In the entrepreneurial phase, *everyone* in the company serves on

What Once Came Naturally...

	In most big companies...	In the start-up *or* World-Class company...
Communication from customers is	Complaint or problem based	Ongoing, multidimensional, and solicited
Customer data are gathered by	Strategists or specialists	The total organization, with a lead assigned to service providers
Responsibility for service belongs to	The customer service department	The total organization
Customer problems are solved	Using strict preset policies and procedures	By service providers empowered to act
Customer needs are interpreted by	Strategists, specialists, or top levels of management	The total organization
Feedback mechanisms are	Preset and static	Ongoing and dynamic
Service is defined by	Complaints or problems	Continuous improvement based on customer data

the front lines. Everyone knows what's going on, what's working, and what's not. Feedback doesn't come in the form of numbers crunched by a researcher. It blasts into your ear when an angry customer calls to give you hell; it serenades your eyes when a letter of praise or a hard-won sales order crosses your desk. Each morning, you rise knowing that you may please your customers or you may disappoint them. And each evening, you lie down with a pretty good idea of how the day transpired.

Further, the entrepreneur *owns* success and failure. You and your small tribe of devoted colleagues are the whole story. There are no layers of bureaucracy to blame, no calcified policies and procedures to hide behind. You act on your best intentions and instincts, doing what you can to make customers happy. It's scary at times. But you are keenly aware of the fact that you're alive.

Something happens to companies as they grow. Gradually, they exchange intimacy with their customers for the security and order of size. They also tend to break up into functional specialties, which increase efficiency, but at a price. "When all you're asked to think about is *your* task or your specific segment of the overall operation," says Tom Oliver, chief operating officer of Federal Express, "it's easy to forget that your real job is making customers happy."

World-class leaders understand that as companies grow, they must actively pursue the closeness to customers that once came naturally.

L.L. Bean, the famed retailer of outdoor clothing and recreational products, is a good example of a company that has managed to stay close to its customers while growing to international prominence.

"Our Customer statement has been around for decades," notes Bob Peixotto, L.L. Bean's vice president of total quality management. "It's something 'L.L.' himself said frequently."

When we asked Peixotto how the statement is used, he said, "The statement is not so much 'used' as 'lived.' People here have really institutionalized customer commitment as a way of life." This is a wonderful thing to be able to say about one's company. And, given Bean's well-earned reputation for doing anything and everything to

"A customer is the most important person ever in this office—in person or by mail. A customer is not dependent on us, we are dependent on him. A customer is not an interruption of our work, he is the purpose of it. We are not doing him a favor by serving him, he is doing us a favor by giving us the opportunity to do so. A customer is not someone to argue or match wits with. Nobody ever won an argument with a customer. A customer is a person who brings us his wants. It is our job to handle them profitably to him and to ourselves."

make customers happy, we were prepared to leave it at that.

But Peixotto had more to say: "I don't want to give anybody the idea that we're living in the past or that we're content to stay the way we are," he stressed. "This company really did grow up on customer focus. But much of our reputation for unlimited customer satisfaction was earned on the basis of *fixing* problems. In fact, we became world-class fixers. Today, we recognize that it would be better for our customers and more productive for us if we did more things right the first time. We work very hard now to *prevent* quality problems from occurring in the first place."

Expressed in terms of the three voices, L.L. Bean was remarkably successful in maintaining company-wide contact with The Voice of the Customer despite its growth. However, the need to fix problems indicates that the company had lost touch with The Voice of the Process.

L.L. Bean is implementing total quality management today primarily to address process issues. And we feel certain that, with its customer-focused tradition *and* its clear commitment to continuous improvement, L.L. Bean will remain among the world's most admired and most loved companies for many years to come.

THE VOICE OF THE EMPLOYEE

Federal Express has a wonderfully concise corporate philosophy: People-Service-Profit. What's more, the sequence of those three elements is no accident. Managers throughout Federal Express are taught to first think in terms of their employees.

"Take care of our people," counsels the Federal Express Manager's Guide. "They, in turn, will deliver the impeccable service demanded by our customers who will reward us with the profitability to secure our future. People-Service-Profit: These three words are the very foundation of Federal Express."

This "People First" management philosophy dates back to the mid-1970s, when Fred Smith launched his company and, in effect, defined a new industry.

Smith first articulated the idea that became Federal Express while a student at Yale. His paper noted that the existing airfreight system served customers poorly. Freight forwarders picked up a package, found a passenger airline's regularly scheduled flight going to the package's destination, and arranged delivery on the other end. It was a catch-as-catch-can system, not terribly reliable, and very slow. It took three or four days for packages to reach their destination although the actual flight time was just a few hours.

Young Smith suggested that a single company could control everything. It would own its own planes, employ its own couriers, and provide everything else required to move a package from point A to point B. What's more, his company would do the job overnight.

Couriers would pick up freight anywhere in the U.S., Smith elaborated, and put it onto planes that would all fly to a single central processing point. At this processing hub, the parcels would be batched that night and put onto the company's outgoing planes for delivery to regional hubs, where couriers would be waiting to deliver customers' packages to any destination in the country.

Smith's professor commented that the scheme would be great for customers, but that regulators would never allow it. He gave the paper a C+.

Fortunately, Smith went ahead with his plan anyway. And, as any senior manager at the company will tell you, the *people* of Federal Express make it work.

"The early years were exciting but extraordinarily difficult," recalls Tom Oliver. "The company's venture capital, as you might expect, was invested primarily in airplanes. Our massive start-up costs did not leave much cash to meet other expenses or to hedge against the early operating losses that confront nearly all new ventures. Money was so tight, in fact, that employees were sometimes asked to wait a week or more before cashing their paychecks. And Federal Express pilots sometimes paid for their aviation fuel out of their own pockets.

"Our people got the company through those difficult times," Oliver says. "Their spirit shaped Federal Express. And our continuing 'People First' management approach demonstrates that we have not forgotten where we came from," he concludes.

True enough. But even at Federal Express, management came dangerously close to losing touch with The Voice of the Employee. John Cahill works out of the Federal Express depot in Bedford, Massachusetts. He has been a Federal Express courier since 1974, when the company served just eleven metropolitan areas and its New England "office" was a back corridor at Hanscom Field, an Air Force base in Massachusetts that allowed a small amount of civil air traffic. Not surprisingly, Cahill thinks of 1974 to 1979 as the "glory days" of Federal Express.

"Starting out, I was presented with this challenge: 'They're laughing at you, John. Go out and beat them.' And I really responded to that," he says. "I'd see a package going Airborne and I'd say to the guy, 'Let me put a Federal label on that and it will get there tomorrow.'"

The hustling employee attitude typified by John Cahill surely helped drive demand for Fred Smith's "C+" air express service concept. In fact, demand skyrocketed, and the company was soon hiring new people by the dozens.

As the company soared into its second decade of unbridled growth, there was little time to transmit the vision and values of Federal Express to newcomers. Everyone was too busy getting the work done, which may explain why some couriers who joined the company between 1980 and 1985 experienced a less inspiring indoctrination than the one recalled by Cahill.

"I felt like I had handcuffs on," recalls Tony Fiore, a former auto mechanic who joined Federal Express at the Bedford depot in 1981. "So many things were going on that didn't make sense. You had to ask yourself, 'Why are they doing this?'"

Fiore says that the Bedford operation still looked like a well-oiled machine to Federal Express customers. But for employees, it was often chaotic. As more and more customers signed on with Federal Express, new couriers were hired and quickly thrown into the fray. Managers, feeling the stress of the company's commitment to "absolutely, positively" meet its obligation to the customer, increasingly barked out orders and squelched employee input. "They were even pulling couriers off a route and sending somebody else in to make some stops, when the person already in the area could have made the stops in a minute," he recalls.

Fiore was far from alone in his growing disillusionment. Cahill recalls that "we were becoming like the government. It was very structured." Federal Express was still getting packages to destinations on time, but couriers didn't sell or deliver service like the old Federal Express people. And in the haste of the daily routine, few gave much thought to controlling costs.

By 1987, Federal Express executives were startled by mounting evidence that the vaunted synergy between Federal Express managers and employees was slipping away. Data from Survey-Feedback-Action, the formal process by which Federal Express gathers and acts on employee input showed that, with each new year, the average employee had a lower opinion of his or her boss.

Survey-Feedback-Action (SFA) is serious business at Federal Express. Employees rate their managers on fairness, receptiveness to input, respectfulness, and many other issues that are important to everyone who works for a living. Each employee also rates upper management's performance in terms of the guidance and direction it provides and its receptivity to new ideas and suggestions. Finally, employees are asked to rate how satisfactorily management addressed the concerns they identified in the previous year's SFA.

Not so different from your company's employee survey? Perhaps. But it's what happens *after* employees complete the surveys that makes SFA special.

At Federal Express, managers are explicitly required to work with their employees to fully understand the legitimate issues and concerns communicated through SFA. What's more, they are expected to resolve those concerns. The surveys are not an end in themselves but a mechanism to trigger problem-solving dialogues between managers and the people who work for them.

And that, of course, brings us to a vital lesson about The Voice of the Employee. As Federal Express grew rapidly out of its entrepreneurial phase and became a major corporation, the vertical lines of communication between management and employees were

SURVEY

A standard, anonymous questionnaire is given to every employee each year. This survey parallels the first step of the FADE (an acronym for focus, analyze, develop, and execute) process of quality improvement—gathering data to focus on the problems and opportunities of a work group. Questions are designed to gather information about what helps and hinders employees in their work environment. Your work group's survey results are calculated and then returned to you.

FEEDBACK

To understand the meaning of the survey results, you must question your work group. The goal of the feedback meeting is to identify specific concerns or problems (FOCUS), examine specific causes for these problems (ANALYZE), and create plans to correct these problems (DEVELOP).

ACTION

The outcome of the feedback meeting should be the development of a Quality Action Plan. This is a list of clear, concise actions to be taken to address concerns and to lead to improved results. Since failing to act on your work group's ideas and concerns creates frustration and disillusionment, taking decisive action enhances your effectiveness and improves your team's results.

```
                                        WORKGROUP  #  10000
ORGANIZATION NAME                          ②
LSTNAME, FIRSTNAME     MANAGEMENT LEVEL
AIRPORT ID        DEPARTMENT                 PERCENT              ④
N = 8             MAY 1, 1990          ①    SOMTIME    ③         #
                                    FAVORABLE  FAV/UNF  UNFAV  NOANS
```

		① FAVORABLE	PERCENT SOMTIME FAV/UNF	③ UNFAV	④ # NOANS
1.	CAN TELL MY MANAGER WHAT I THINK.	86	14	0	1
2.	MY MANAGER TELLS ME WHAT IS EXPECTED.	86	0	14	1
3.	FAVORITISM NOT A PROBLEM IN MY WORKGROUP. .	57	0	43	1
4.	MY MANAGER HELPS US DO OUR JOB BETTER.	43	29	29	1
5.	MY MANAGER LISTENS TO MY CONCERNS.	86	0	14	1
6.	MY MANAGER ASKS FOR MY IDEAS ABOUT WORK. . .	67	0	33	2
7.	MY MANAGER TELLS ME WHEN I DO A GOOD JOB. . .	100	0	0	1
8.	MY MANAGER TREATS ME WITH RESPECT.	100	0	0	1
9.	MY MANAGER KEEPS ME INFORMED.	83	0	17	2
10.	MY MANAGER DOES NOT INTERFERE WITH JOB. . . .	71	29	0	1
11.	MY MANAGERS BOSS GIVES US SUPPORT WE NEED	50	17	33	2
12.	UPPER MGT TELLS US COMPANY GOALS.	50	33	17	2
13.	UPPER MGT LISTENS TO IDEAS FROM MY LEVEL. . .	0	0	100	2
14.	HAVE CONFIDENCE IN THE FAIRNESS OF MGT.	17	33	50	2
15.	CAN BE SURE OF A JOB IF I DO GOOD WORK.	100	0	0	1
16.	PROUD TO WORK FOR FEDERAL EXPRESS.	100	0	0	1
17.	WORK LEADING TO KIND OF FUTURE I WANT.	100	0	0	2
18.	FED EX DOES A GOOD JOB FOR OUR CUSTOMERS. .	100	0	0	1
19.	WORKING FOR FEDERAL EXPRESS IS A GOOD DEAL	100	0	0	1
20.	PAID FAIRLY FOR THIS KIND OF WORK.	57	0	43	1
21.	BENEFIT PROGRAMS MEET MOST OF MY NEEDS. . .	100	0	0	1
22.	PEOPLE COOPERATE WITHIN THIS WORKGROUP. . .	100	0	0	1
23.	THERE IS COOPERATION BETWEEN WORKGROUPS.	86	14	0	1
24.	IN MY ENVIR. WE USE SAFE WORK PRACTICES. . . .	100	0	0	2
25.	RULES AND PROCEDURES DO NOT INTERFERE. . . .	43	14	43	1
26.	ABLE TO GET SUPPLIES AND RESOURCES.	86	0	14	1
27.	HAVE ENOUGH FREEDOM TO DO MY JOB WELL. . . .	100	0	0	1
28.	WKGRP INVOLVED IN IMPROVING SVC TO CUSTMRS	100	0	0	3
29.	1989 SFA CONCERNS WERE ADDRESSED SATISF. . .	33	17	50	2

```
⑤ → SFA AVERAGE PERCENT FAVORABLE    76
⑥ → IR INDEX =                        71
⑦ → LEADERSHIP INDEX =                78
⑧ → LEADERSHIP AVG =                  3.8
```

	① FAVORABLE	PERCENT SOMTIME FAV/UNF	③ UNFAV	④ # NOANS
LOCAL QUESTION 1.	33	17	50	2
LOCAL QUESTION 2.	100	0	0	2
LOCAL QUESTION 3.	0	0	100	4
LOCAL QUESTION 4.	33	17	50	2
LOCAL QUESTION 5.	33	33	33	2
LOCAL QUESTION 6.	33	33	33	2
LOCAL QUESTION 7.	60	0	40	3
LOCAL QUESTION 8.	50	17	33	2
LOCAL QUESTION 9.	71	0	29	1
LOCAL QUESTION 10.	100	0	0	7

1990 Survey Feedback Action

predictably strained. As a direct result, the camaraderie and esprit de corps that characterized Federal Express were in jeopardy.

However, unlike the leaders of most other large companies, the executives at Federal Express *knew* what was happening with their employees. They had SFA: an established, credible, reliable mechanism for accessing what once came naturally—The Voice of the Employee. SFA warned the leaders of Federal Express that a dark shadow lurked behind the white light of their company's phenomenal growth.

Federal Express also explicitly motivated its managers to act on what the SFA scores told them. Individual advancement at Federal Express has always been dependent, in part, on receiving high SFA scores from one's employees and on demonstrating the willingness and ability to solve the problems that hinder employee effectiveness. But when average SFA ratings started to slip in the late 1980s, Federal Express adopted a new approach. It made its managers *collectively* responsible for raising the overall SFA rating. Beginning in 1989, a significant part of every manager's compensation—including that of senior executives—was tied directly to reaching the company-wide SFA improvement goal. If the goal isn't met, managers forgo that compensation, even if their own individual SFA score is high.

Thus, Federal Express has used SFA to drive fundamental improvements in its management culture. Managers study the SFA data because they are rewarded for listening to employees and for adopting the behaviors of those managers who consistently earn the highest SFA ratings. This concerted effort to hear and respond to The Voice of the Employee was launched in the context of a comprehensive total quality management implementation aimed not only at resolving employee concerns, but at strengthening the company's ties to The Voice of the Customer and The Voice of the Process as well.

The result is a renewed entrepreneurial spirit. Federal Express has recaptured the sense of excitement, involvement, and challenge that inspired veterans like John Cahill in the early days. The curve of SFA scores has turned upward once more and continues to improve with each passing year. Not coincidentally, Federal Express became the first service company to be honored with the Malcolm Baldrige National Quality Award.[1] And the innumerable customer-focused quality improvements generated by Federal Express employees have clearly strengthened the company during its difficult and sometimes perilous period of international expansion.

THE VOICE OF THE PROCESS

We have suggested that as companies grow, employees can lose the entrepreneur's natural intimacy with customers. Further, the leaders of growing companies are often distanced from The Voice of the Employee by the lengthening chain of command. A third fundamental truth about post-entrepreneurial organizations is that their people can lose touch with *how work gets done.*

It is difficult for an individual to relate to the macro-operations of a 1,000-employee company, let alone those of a General Motors. The sheer mass of such organizations makes employees feel powerless, as do the multiple layers through which their work must pass before reaching customers. Can anything one person does really make a difference?

Of course, employees *want* to make a difference. They long to see evidence that their actions have consequences. Therefore, as an organization grows, employees tend to become more focused on their own immediate tasks and to lose sight of the larger work process. This, in turn, leads to significant variance in standards and performance as different parts of the company and even individual employees develop their own parochial views of what constitutes quality.

Managers design the work processes in which employees complete their tasks and are responsible for overall work performance. So one might assume that managers understand the inner workings of the processes under their command. But the truth is, they usually don't.

The experience of Milliken & Company, the remarkable textile manufacturer based in Spartanburg, South Carolina, illustrates why hearing and responding to The Voice of the Process is so fundamental to competitive success.

"The most important event in Milliken's quality journey took place in 1979," says Darryl Jackson, an executive who rapidly advanced up Milliken & Company's management ranks from 1980 to 1988. "That was the year Roger Milliken (founder and CEO) and his top executives went over to Japan."

Today, Jackson is chief operating officer of M.S. Carriers, a Memphis-based transportation firm. But in 1979, he was a fresh-faced, twenty-seven-year-old strategic planning analyst, the newest addition to the firm's corporate staff. The fates had placed Jackson where he would witness, and participate in, the company-wide transformation that ensued upon Roger Milliken's return from the Far East.

"Mr. Milliken and his top managers went over there because some Japanese textile firms were just beating our brains out in terms of quality, price, and value. And that was pretty darn perplexing because, at Milliken, we had the best machinery and technology, the best research and development, the best of everything," Jackson says. Milliken was, in fact, the clear quality leader in the United States. Yet quality levels in the best Japanese mills were running several fold better than what Milliken could generate in terms of defect level per-hundred-yards.

In Japan, the Milliken group encountered "these little plants that, next to ours, looked like holes in the wall," Jackson reports.

"Their equipment was unbelievably antiquated. Nothing our executives saw over there measured up to what we had back home. Mr. Milliken scratched his head and said, 'What in the heck's going on here?'" The Milliken executives delved into the mystery and soon found the answer: startlingly effective management of work processes.

"The management of work processes in the Japanese textile mills was virtually flawless. The people in the chain of work simply made no mistakes," Jackson says. "Their workers were weighing out dye on these primitive scales. Yet the dye distribution on the fabric was perfect.

"We had all these wonderful machines to do what they were doing manually, but they were still beating us on quality tenfold," Jackson summarizes. "There was just no way we could go on depending on superior technology to keep us ahead. We were already behind."

Jackson feels certain that these revelations affected Roger Milliken. "I've often thought how hard it must have been for him," Jackson says. "He'd been running this very successful company for thirty-five years, always pushing for improvement and always determined to make his company the quality leader. He decided what the company would do to achieve quality. Then everyone else, like good soldiers, went out and did it."

But the Far East trip convinced Roger Milliken that a large company involves too many processes for one talented executive, or even a whole team of talented executives, to manage alone. Every manager *and* employee must be attuned to The Voice of the Process to produce quality at the levels then attained by overseas competitors.

"Mr. Milliken was the first one to say 'Maybe I've been going at this wrong.' That must have been a tough thing for him to admit. But he did," Jackson says. "From that point on, nobody pushed harder than Roger Milliken to get more people involved and to turn over more responsibilities to the people who do the work. Instead of being the experts who solved every problem, managers were then required to prepare their people to understand, control, and improve the company's work processes. That was our new job. And Mr. Milliken made it clear there was no turning back."

Jackson soon had opportunity to try out Milliken's new management approach on the front lines. "Not long after I arrived, they threw me to the wolves as a first line supervisor. I swung shifts for about nine months, managing guys twice my age," he says. Jackson experimented with some of the process management approaches then introduced in the company and worked hard to involve the employees under his supervision in quality improvement. The workers responded and quality on his shifts improved dramatically.

Shortly thereafter, Jackson was named plant manager of Milliken's New Holland facility in Gainesville, Georgia. It was a huge step up for a supervisor with less than two years' experience. He took it as a sign that he should continue with his experimentation in quality management.

Though better than average by U.S. standards, the Gainesville mill was then among the worst in Milliken for quality. Jackson and his supervisors worked with employees to flowchart key work processes, asked workers to analyze and make constant adjustments in their operating procedures, and urged everyone to continuously question the established work processes, just in case a better way was available.

In less than a year, the New Holland mill went from producing 8 percent to less than 1 percent off-quality product. And actual efficiency of the plant's machinery increased from 86 percent to 94 percent—a rate higher than the manufacturer said was possible.

Jackson stresses that his successful experience at New Holland was a small part of a major quality success story that included, among many other components, "a massive movement toward total customer satisfaction" that began in 1982 and an extraordinarily successful employee suggestion system. Milliken & Company was selected as a winner of the 1989 Malcolm Baldrige National Quality Award.

Perhaps even more gratifying than winning the Baldrige Award, however, was the comment of a Japanese auto executive. After a tour of Milliken's plants to evaluate the company as a supplier of upholstery fabrics for his company's automobiles, he told his hosts "Milliken is more like a Japanese company than a Japanese company." It was intended as a supreme compliment. Milliken & Company won that contract, and since then has won many more from Japanese customers.

Startled by the success of foreign competitors, Roger Milliken empowered his 13,000 managers and employees to tap into The Voice of the Process and regain control over how work gets done. Milliken focused first on process data, then balanced that focus with emphases on The Voice of the Customer and The Voice of the Employee. Today, Milliken & Company can match quality with any competitor in the world.

Conclusion

Fred Smith and Roger Milliken are visionaries—leaders of extraordinary ability. In many ways, their actions demonstrate what we mean by world-class leadership.

However, leaders need not be world-*famous* to be world-*class*. Nor must they be chief executives. As Darryl Jackson demonstrated, the same leadership principles can be applied at the supervisory and middle-management levels. Further, world-class leaders do not necessarily exude movie star charisma or work for one of the "blue chip" corporations regularly mentioned in business books.

There is far more commonality in what world-class leaders *do* than in who they are.

World-class leaders understand the fundamental changes that occur in organizations as they grow. They recognize that their job is to regain the natural advantages of the entrepreneurial company—intimacy with the customer, strong communication links between leaders and those they lead, and a firm grasp of work processes by every employee—without sacrificing growth or the advantages of size.

To accomplish this mission, world-class leaders are always prepared to change and to demand change of others. They build systems and shape corporate culture that enable their large companies to truly hear and respond to The Voice of the Customer, The Voice of the Employee, and The Voice of the Process.

In the following chapters, we will explore in greater detail how world-class leaders constantly balance these three voices. But first, let's pause to consider *why* you should study this approach to business leadership. That is, let's appraise the potential benefits of making quality work for you and your organization.

NOTE

1. Instituted by the U.S. Congress in 1987, the Malcolm Baldrige National Quality Award recognizes quality achievement and excellence. All privately or publicly held companies incorporated and located in the U.S. are eligible for the award, which includes categories for manufacturing, service, and small business corporations. For more information on the Baldrige Award, see Appendix B.

4 ■ QUALITY: "THE UNFAIR ADVANTAGE"

DILBERT by Scott Adams

DILBERT reprinted by permission of UFS, INC.

In a 1988 interview, we asked Jim Robinson, then chairman of American Express, why he pushed so hard for quality improvement in a company that the business press was already calling "the quintessence of profitable consumerism." Robinson smiled at us and said, "I enjoy having an unfair competitive advantage."

Of course, no advantage is more "fair" than a reputation for quality. And no advantage is more difficult to earn and maintain (as Robinson himself would tell you). What the Amex chairman was *really* saying, in playful terms, is that the cumulative benefits of a quality-based advantage are so powerful that competitors have little chance of overcoming them to defeat you in the marketplace.

For us, this is an article of faith. We are utterly convinced that organizations that successfully differentiate themselves on the basis of quality will become lions in the modern global marketplace. The best of them will stand virtually unchallenged, frightening off any and all hungry wolves hoping to prey upon their customer base.

Still, we recognize that not all readers share our conviction. As

Voltaire said, "The world needs skeptics, not cynics." Since good business people are notoriously skeptical, we'll offer four cases to support our contention that quality *is* "the unfair advantage."

THE RESEARCH CASE

For those who trust only what can be expressed in numbers, we point to a growing body of convincing research. The landmark Profit Impact of Market Strategy (PIMS) project, for example, documented the link between customer perception of quality and a company's financial performance and market share.

To create the PIMS data base, researchers from the Strategic Planning Institute (SPI) of Cambridge, Massachusetts, worked in cooperation with Harvard University to obtain detailed, confidential data on more than 3,000 business units in 450 companies. The sample represented all major sectors of the economy.

The SPI's "quality profiling" approach asked managers within these companies to rate their own company's products or service attributes, and those of their principal competitors, against criteria which they deemed important to customers (The Voice of the Customer). The judgmental ratings assigned by the managers were then tested against ratings gathered directly from customers and, when appropriate, modified.

The PIMS data base documented that businesses ranked in the top fifth for "perceived quality" enjoyed, on average, a pretax return on investment of more than 30 percent a year. In contrast, businesses ranked in the bottom two-fifths for perceived quality achieved an average pretax return on investment of just 16 percent. In other words, the highly regarded business units out-earned their less respected peers by an average margin of two to one.[1]

The SPI researchers identified similar correlations between perceived quality and return on sales and perceived quality and business growth. In *The PIMS Principles: Linking Strategy to Perfor-*

mance, Drs. Robert Buzzell and Bradley Gale summarized the SPI's conclusions on the link between customer perceptions of quality and competitiveness:

> Achieving superior perceived quality gives your business three options—all of them good. First, you can charge a higher price for your superior quality offering and let the premium fall right to the bottom line. Second, you can charge a higher price and invest the premium in R&D and in new products to ensure your perceived quality and market share for the future. Third, you can offer the customer better value by charging the same price as competitors, but for your superior product/service offering. The gain in share means volume growth, rising capacity utilization and, ultimately, capacity expansion allowing you to introduce new equipment that embodies the latest cost-saving technology.[2]

Buzzell and Gale also note the competitive advantages of achieving what SPI calls "conformance quality," or the degree to which company performance measures up to its own specifications, expectations, and standards (The Voice of the Process).

> Achieving superior conformance quality yields two key benefits. First, it means a lower cost of quality than that of competitors, and thereby a lower overall cost. Second, conformance quality is often one of the key attributes that count in the purchase decision. So achieving superior conformance quality yields both lower cost and superior perceived quality, a double benefit.[3]

We would add that the PIMS research focused primarily on customer perceptions of product or service offerings. If SPI had also explored the role of *relationships* in perceived quality—that is, if they had also focused on how companies and customers interact—

we believe the findings would have been more dramatic still.

The PIMS results were corroborated in May 1991, when the U.S. General Accounting Office published the results of its review of twenty companies that were among the highest-scoring applicants in 1988 and 1989 for the Malcolm Baldrige National Quality Award.

The GAO concluded that these companies had significantly improved their performance through quality efforts. "In nearly all cases," the report stated, "companies that used total quality management practices achieved better employee relations, higher productivity, greater customer satisfaction, increased market share, and improved profitability."[4]

In fact, we have witnessed an avalanche of research findings substantiating the links between quality, customer retention, and business success, some with particularly hard-hitting messages for business leaders:

• The American Management Association estimates that 65 percent of the average company's business comes from its *repeat* customers.[5]

• Research conducted for the Office of Consumer Affairs indicates that 91 percent of dissatisfied customers will never do business with the offending company again.[6]

• Technical Assistance Research Programs of Washington, D.C., estimates that it costs five times more to attract a new customer than it does to retain an old one.[7]

When you boil it all down, we believe that this research (while valuable) serves mainly to provide empirical confirmation of a truth business leaders have always understood: Customers are like fine antique china. They must never be dropped.

THE ALIGNMENT CASE

For intuitive thinkers, we find the most powerful way to illustrate that quality *is* "the unfair advantage" is through a diagram we first shared with executives at Procter & Gamble.

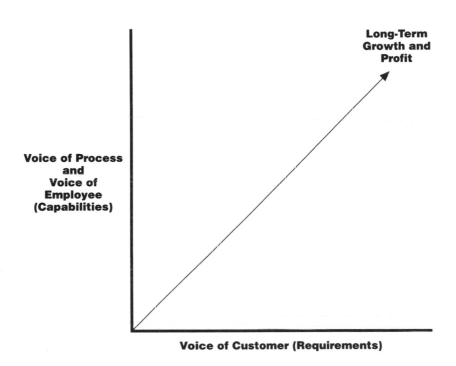

The vertical axis represents the ongoing development of your organization's capabilities—its employees and work processes. The horizontal axis represents the advance of your customers' requirements. The middle arrow represents your organization's overall performance in terms of long-term growth and profitability.

When your organization's capabilities are equal to the demands placed on it by customers, The Voice of the Employee and The Voice of the Process are aligned with The Voice of the Customer.

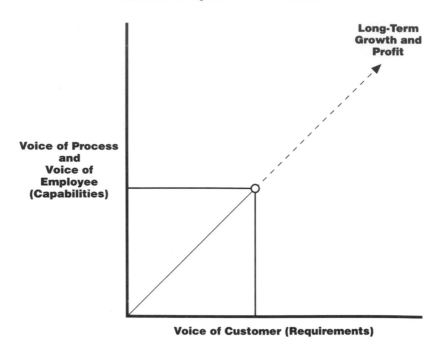

The relationship is steady and your growth and profitability advance at a moderately healthy pace.

Should your capabilities lag behind customer requirements, however, The Voice of the Employee and The Voice of the Process fall out of alignment with The Voice of the Customer, and you are confronted with a Rework Gap.

Your organization can't routinely satisfy its customers and must go to extraordinary lengths (e.g., recall and repair of defective products or "make good" on services delivered unsatisfactorily) just to sustain the relationship. As you can see, growth and profitability suffer.

Once the Rework Gap has been closed, your organization may move out of alignment in the other direction—your capabilities might run *ahead* of customers' current requirements. When this happens, you create what we call an Opportunity Gap. Your orga-

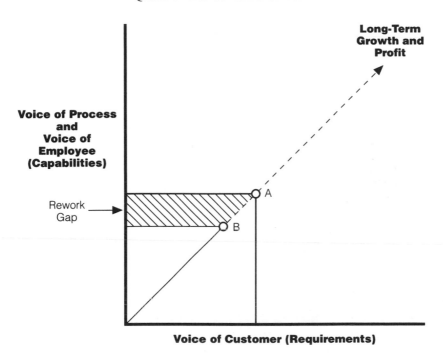

nization not only routinely satisfies customers' current requirements, it is ready and able to meet needs that customers have not yet stated or, perhaps, even imagined.

We must stress that the Opportunity Gap is *not* about "gold plating" or hanging useless "bells and whistles" on already functional products. Nor is it about supplier-driven advances in technology that put your organization in the uncomfortable position of trying to convince customers that they want what you have to offer. Rather, the Opportunity Gap represents your organization's ability to make insightful, educated guesses about customers' unstated and anticipated needs, so you can provide unexpected elements of product, service, or relationship quality that customers will immediately and intrinsically *value*. It is about "delighting" customers, as opposed to merely satisfying them. Most of all, it is about leading the marketplace, as opposed to following it.

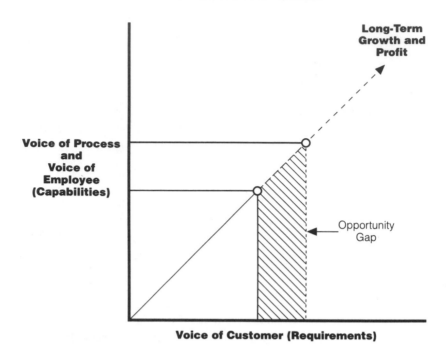

For example, all competent home builders pay attention to the durability and conformity of the bricks used in their projects. But the builder who wishes to stand apart may also choose to use only bricks that weather in a way that is aesthetically pleasing to the homeowner. This source of delight may not be evident to customers until years after they purchase their new homes. But over time, the enhanced level of satisfaction such unexpected "extras" generate will set this one builder apart in the marketplace as a quality supplier.

In terms of competitive advantage, we see that organizations actually pursue two kinds of quality goals. Defensive quality goals are reactive. They are aimed at closing the Rework Gap—bringing process and employee capabilities up to par with customer requirements. Rather than leading the marketplace, the organization is trying to catch up with it. When the organization opens up an

Opportunity Gap, however, it can proactively pursue Offensive quality goals that will favorably distance it from competitors in the mind of the marketplace, drive customer retention and new business growth, and lessen pressures to compete on the basis of price, thereby increasing long-term profitability.

We'll return to this central issue of alignment in later chapters, but we'll leave the subject here with one important caution: Once your organization "delights" its customers with unexpected value, their base requirements will rise to this new level of expectation. The dotted line becomes solid, indicating that The Voice of the Process and The Voice of the Employee are again in alignment with The Voice of the Customer, albeit at a new, higher level.

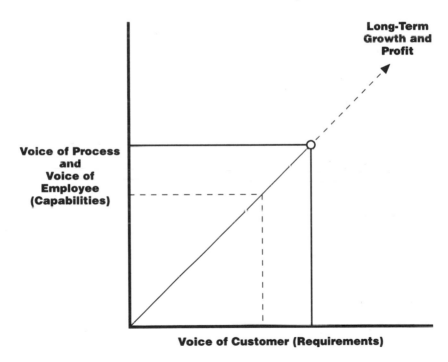

Like the Olympic high jumper who sets a new world record, you have forever "raised the bar." From now on, *this* is the level of performance and value your customers will expect from you.

On the plus side, you have also raised your rate of growth and profitability. And in all likelihood, your customers will demand at least the same level of performance from your competitors, who will be forced to focus on Defensive quality goals to close the Rework Gap you have created for them. Your organization, meanwhile, will have the luxury of pursuing a new Opportunity Gap and focusing on a whole new set of Offensive quality goals.

The Experiential Case: Personal Quality Audit

Here's a quick pencil and paper exercise you can use to evaluate the quality of your own work and assess your level of contribution to your organization's overall quality advantage.

Step 1. Consider that every job has two dimensions: *What you do* and *How you do it.*

• *What you do* falls into one of two categories: Right Things and Wrong Things
• *How you do work* also falls into two categories: Things Done Right and Things Done Wrong

Step 2. Now, combine these dimensions into a four-block grid.

Step 3. List on a separate sheet of paper the *major* work activities in which you've been engaged during the last two weeks. (Feel free to consult your calendar.) Examples: attended planning conference, ordered new equipment, developed business proposal.

Step 4. Review your list. Write each of the activities you listed in the appropriate box of the four-block grid. (This example might help you make your selections.)

How You Do It →

■ **STEP 2** ■

Right Things Wrong	**Right Things Right**
Wrong Things Wrong	**Wrong Things Right**

What You Do ↑

How You Do It →

■ **STEP 4** ■

Right Things Wrong	**Right Things Right**
• Installed service as requested on schedule, but connected incorrectly • Filled out correct form, but information inaccurate	• Completed necessary report correctly and on schedule • Provided information as requested by customer in an accurate, timely manner
Wrong Things Wrong	**Wrong Things Right**
• Scheduled unnecessary meeting, poorly run • Sent bill to wrong person, calculation incorrect	• Ordered wrong equipment, but installed correctly • Completed report not requested by the customer, but written well and submitted on time

What You Do ↑

Step 5. Estimate the percentage of your *time* spent on the activities listed in each square of the grid.

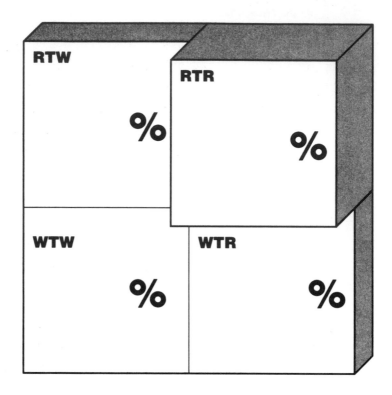

Step 6. Subtract your Right Things Right (RTR) percentage from 100 percent.

100% − _____ **% =** _____ **%**

(Total)   (RTR)   (Avoidable Cost
of Quality)

How much of your time was spent on activities other than those that were Right Things Right?

We find that, on average, individuals spend *approximately 55 percent of their time doing Right Things Right.* A client of ours once quipped that, at a 55 percent rate of quality performance, everyone in his company might just as well stay home two days a week. The problem with that solution, of course, is that no one knows *which* two days are being wasted.

Instead, consider how much more you (and the people who work for you) might accomplish *without working harder* if only you could spend more of your time doing the Right Things Right. How might increasing that percentage a mere 10 percent affect your personal performance? If such an improvement was achieved across your work force, how would that affect your organization's ability to reduce waste and rework, cut costs, and favorably impress customers?

A "Real-World" Case

Finally, for those who believe only in what is proven in the real world, under non-laboratory conditions we offer the story of CSX Transportation.

CSX Transportation of Jacksonville, Florida, is America's largest railroad (in terms of revenue), with 18,800 miles of track stretching from the Atlantic and Gulf coasts west to the Mississippi and north to Canada. CSXT is also America's oldest operating rail system. Today its trains carry freight over lines established as early as 1827 by CSXT predecessor companies.

But not even 150 years of railroad experience could prepare CSX Transportation for the tumultuous events of the 1980s. In 1980, the storied Chessie System merged with the Seaboard Coast Line to form CSX, the parent corporation of today's CSX Transportation. In that same year, Ronald Reagan was elected President, and the transportation industry braced for the shock of a new government hell-bent on deregulation.

"The government had set interstate transportation rates for as long as anybody could remember," explains Dale Hawk, Vice President–Sales (formerly Vice President–Quality) at CSX Transportation. "Regulation had desensitized us somewhat from the needs of our customers, since we had little room to customize our services to meet specific customer requirements. Of course, regulation also shielded railroads like ours from a large block of potential competitors. The rates the government stipulated for railroads were often much more affordable than those they mandated for shipping the same kinds of freight by truck."

With deregulation, however, hundreds of hungry trucking companies were suddenly free to compete for the railroads' freight business. The sudden impact of open competition hit the entire rail industry—including CSXT—hard, triggering a severe downward spiral.

CSX Transportation downsized dramatically during the 1980s. Nearly 9,000 track miles were cut from the previous 28,000, and the employee population was reduced by more than half, from a high of 73,000 to less than 34,000 today. Although much of that downsizing was a conscious response to suddenly adverse market conditions, by 1985 the company was looking for ways to reverse the trend and resume healthy, sustainable growth.

In the years following 1985, a few critical events spurred a remarkable quality awakening within CSX Transportation.

"For the first time in the company's history, we conducted formal customer research interviews," Hawk reports. "We learned that a lot of customers actually disliked doing business with our railroad, which was a pretty sobering fact when you consider how many other options were open to them."

"QUALITY CASCADE"
These research findings were soon followed by a straightforward lesson in the role of quality in business success, delivered personally by representatives of Amoco, one of CSX Transportation's most important customers.

"The folks from Amoco really laid it on the line," Hawk says "They weren't criticizing us so much as trying to help us understand how much was at stake."

The Amoco people described what Hawk terms a "Quality Cascade" in which the performance of CSX Transportation strongly influenced the success or failure of five other companies. Hawk explains: "At the top of the quality cascade was Ford Motor Company, which by this time had gotten very serious about improving quality. Ford was demanding that its upholstery supplier provide better seat covers for its cars, at lower costs and with more dependable deliveries.

"The upholsterer, in turn, looked to Monsanto Chemical to deliver higher quality fibers, at lower costs, and with more dependable deliveries. Of course, Monsanto then passed the same quality demands down the cascade to its own supplier, Celanese, which provided chemicals Monsanto used to manufacture its fiber. After that, Celanese demanded improved feed stocks, delivered more dependably and at lower costs from CSXT's customer, Amoco.

"By this point in the conversation, we knew why the Amoco folks were there. They said 'We can make the best terephthalic acid in the world, but if you deliver it late to Celanese, we're going to lose their business.' Nobody had to tell us that if we caused Amoco to lose a key customer, an apology and a refund wouldn't be enough to make amends," Hawk concludes.

Confronted with the disturbing results of the customer interviews and the growing demands of Amoco and other customers, John Snow, then president of the railroad and now chairman, president, and CEO of CSX Corporation, led an all-out effort to transform CSX Transportation into a railroad that could delight its customers and fend off the rash of new competitors. Snow directed a hands-on senior management study of twenty-six American companies known for quality, including Ford, Dow Chemical, IBM,

Baltimore Gas & Electric, Hewlett-Packard, and 3M. He sent teams of two or three CSXT senior managers to see what could be learned from each firm.

The CSXT executives returned with a message that Hawk summarizes in five fundamental points:

"Quality is free." The slogan had been popularized six years earlier by Philip Crosby. Based on what they saw and heard in their visits, Snow's senior management team was now convinced that it is always more expensive to run out-of-control work processes than it is to invest in quality approaches designed to bring work processes under control.

"Quality is a management problem." Poor quality is not caused by lazy workers, but by flawed management systems. And if managers were the problem, then managers would also have to lead the way to solutions.

"The company must focus everything on customers." The CSXT executives were particularly impressed by the concept of "internal customers" that required employees who never saw a bill-paying customer to think of fellow employees as customers. By meeting fellow employees' valid customer requirements, everyone could help CSX Transportation meet the needs of the external customers served by the company.

"Quality is continuous improvement." The status quo is never good enough. Quality companies constantly strive to be better, and gladly accept that their efforts to improve quality will never end.

"Quality requires culture change." Don't bother looking for quick-fixes or shortcuts, the CSXT executives were told, because there are

none. To achieve meaningful quality improvement, you have to redefine your whole company and change the way every employee views his or her job.

Convinced that these were fundamental truths, CSX Transportation leaders embraced a quality-focused vision of their company's future.

BREAKING IN THE NEW CLERK

CSXT executives next set out to learn more about the inner workings of their company. For example, one key executive spent several days working as a clerk. He studied the procedures manual. To the amusement of his fellow clerks, he then tried to do the job "by the book."

"The career clerks watched the executive struggling to match the procedures in our manual to the realities of the job," Hawk reports. "After a while, I guess they felt kind of sorry for him, because some of them worked up the courage to come over and say, 'Why don't you try doing it this way?' When he put the manual aside and followed their advice, he became a much more effective clerk."

Thus, in addition to systematically hearing The Voice of the Customer through the company's first-ever formal customer interviews, CSXT senior managers took their first concrete steps to tap into The Voice of the Employee, and thereby learned vital truths about their business that no report could tell them.

Just as important, Snow and his fellow executives had demonstrated that they were not, as many employees apparently believed, too elitist to accept change. Their actions symbolized that change was possible, perhaps even inevitable. This, in turn, served to "unfreeze" long-held employee attitudes and assumptions about management and the company.

CSX Transportation then launched a large-scale total quality training effort unlike anything the railroad's employees had experienced before. In fact, management was concerned that its unionized employees would spurn its offer of TQM training. Thousands of workers had recently been "furloughed," which CSXT employees soon understood to be a euphemism for "laid off."

"We were just losing jobs left and right," recalls Joe Fletcher, a veteran trainman. "Management was selling off all our track. And it looked to us like they were trying to just run off business."

However, Fletcher and many of his fellow engineers, conductors, switchmen, signalmen, and field machinists eventually signed on to the management-initiated TQM effort. The leaders of CSX Transportation offered no guarantees that the job losses would end if employees participated in total quality. They could, on the other hand, virtually guarantee that many more furloughs would follow if the company did not free itself from its downward spiral.

Instead of resisting attempts to involve them in improving the company, the employees of CSX Transportation consistently welcomed the opportunity. The values underlying total quality made sense to them. And, at the very least, the TQM training was tangible evidence that CSXT senior management cared about something other than cost-cutting. CSXT management also made special efforts to show union leaders that total quality management was in the long-term interests of labor and management alike.

"We've held thousands of TQM training sessions," Hawk says, "and most of the time, you can't tell which participants are from labor and which are from management. They all act very much the same. I guess it's because they're all there for the same reasons."

The investment in TQM training ensured that the people of CSX Transportation had the skills they needed to do what senior management, already convinced of the need to improve quality, was asking them to do. At last, the company was positioned to advance on all three main fronts of competitive advantage—customer loyalty, employee commitment, and operating efficiency.

New Measures

Hawk reports that the total quality process spurred his company to adopt dramatically new and different measures of performance.

"We'd always tracked locomotive *availability*," he explains. "That, of course, motivated the folks in our repair shops to push out any locomotive capable of pulling a train that day, even if the maintenance work required on that engine wasn't complete. As we studied TQM and heard about the importance of *prevention* in achieving quality, we could see clearly how this measurement approach was standing in the way of us serving our customers," he continues.

CSXT started to track another statistic—mean time between locomotive failures—and to emphasize reliability (rather than availability) to its maintenance staff. Responding to the shift in priorities, the people who maintain CSXT's locomotives soon quadrupled the mean time the company's locomotives ran without failing, from the old standard of twenty days to a new trouble-free performance span of more than eighty days.

In the same vein, Hawk reports that the Customer Focus pillar of quality (see Appendix C) spurred CSXT to de-emphasize "train performance" (the percentage of time its trains arrive at their destinations on schedule) in favor of another measure: "car performance."

"We were very proud that more than 99 percent of our trains pulled in on schedule," he says. "Unfortunately, our customers couldn't care less when the train arrives. What they want to know is when can we produce their *car* at the loading dock. Too often, our trains would arrive at the yard right on schedule, then sit there. Our customers might have to wait several days to actually off-load their property. It was a classic example of how measurements can mislead you," Hawk contended. "Our data showed that we were performing beautifully when, in truth, our customers were bristling at having to wait for us to bring them their cars."

CUSTOMER-FOCUSED RESULTS

Fortunately, CSX Transportation now gives its customers far less reason to bristle. Here is a sampling of the customer-focused quality improvements generated by involved managers and employees throughout CSXT's railroad operations.

• Reduced the time new customers had to wait for processing of credit reports from ninety days to just ten days, then went on to *eliminate* the need to run credit reports for all but a few classes of customers (e.g., small freight forwarders).

• Improved billing accuracy from 88.5 percent in 1986 to 97.5 percent today.

• Reduced personal injuries to employees by 86 percent since launching TQM in 1986.

• Increased the car acceptance ratio (a measure of how many CSXT freight cars are deemed acceptable by customers) to 99.7 percent. This reject rate of less than 1 percent is currently the best in the industry.

• Reduced the average time required to settle customer claims for damaged or missing freight from 69 days at the end of 1987 to less than 25 days by late in 1990.

Clearly, customers have noticed the improvements at CSX Transportation, which has been recognized with a wide array of impressive awards, including:

• LTV Steel's Outstanding Supplier Award (CSX Transportation was the only railroad to receive this honor)

- E.I. duPont's Outstanding Carrier for 1989
- James River Corporation's Gold Key Service Award (its highest symbol of excellence)
- Procter & Gamble's Preferred Quality Carrier
- Monsanto's Preferred Quality Supplier Award
- Union Carbide's Rail Carrier of the Year
- The International Customer Service Association's ICSA Award of Excellence

And what of the folks from Amoco Chemical, whose visit to CSX Transportation in the mid-1980s fueled the railroad's commitment to quality? Amoco is still a valued CSXT customer. In fact, Amoco Chemical recently presented CSX Transportation a Quality Certificate of Accomplishment for overall service performance.

Further, in an industry where employee safety is the paramount concern, CSX Transportation reduced its accident rate by 54 percent and the number of injuries to its personnel by 35 percent in just one year.

Finally, for those skeptics who would say you can't put plaques, certificates, and trophies in the bank, we'll add that the price of CSX stock rose from $26 to $66 per share (late in 1992) after the company embarked on its total quality journey.

CONCLUSION

No matter what lens you apply—quantitative research, intuitive reason, personal experience, or documented performance in the marketplace—the correlation of quality and competitive advantage is clear. Quality *is* "the unfair advantage."

World-class leaders don't dedicate themselves to quality because it's "nice." They do it because they like to *win*. And they know to *keep* winning in an era of global competition, the organizations they lead must be even better tomorrow than they are today. Those who excel in this pursuit of continuous quality improvement will become lions in the marketplace, capable of fending off any and all competitive challenges.

NOTES

1. Robert D. Buzzell and Bradley T. Gale, *The PIMS Principles: Linking Strategy to Performance* (New York: Free Press, 1987).

2. Ibid.

3. Ibid.

4. "Management Practices, U.S. Companies Improve Performance Through Quality Efforts," United States General Accounting Office, May 1991.

5. Harry Bacas, "Make It Right for the Customer," *Nation's Business*, November 1987.

6. Technical Assistance Research Programs (TARP), Washington, D.C.

7. Ibid.

5 ■ FROM CAVEAT EMPTOR TO CUSTOMER-SUPPLIER PARTNERSHIP

DILBERT by Scott Adams

In the last chapter, we suggested that The Voice of the Customer is the one true beacon of competitive advantage. Only your customers can show you the road to long-term growth and profitability.

Admittedly, we are far from the first to preach the importance of "getting close to the customer." But what does "getting close" mean?

Figuratively speaking, it means making effective use of market studies, formal customer research, and continuous informal data gathering to stay attuned to changing customer needs and preferences. Such information is absolutely essential to shape a successful business strategy.

However, when we urge you to "get close," we also mean it literally. Create opportunities to be in the same room with your customers—especially with the leaders of your key customer organizations. Learn how they think and what they believe. Most of all, find out where their needs and aspirations correspond with your own.

Collecting Customer Data: The Pros and Cons

Advantages	Disadvantages
Analysis of Existing Data	
• It may save time and money. • The people who collect the data and those who respect them will accept the data. • You may get information that you would not otherwise have access to.	• The data may be incomplete, unreliable, or out of date. • The data may be difficult to obtain or understand. • The data may be irrelevant to your situation.
Direct Observation	
• You can believe what you see. • You don't have to interpret other people's communications. • You can redirect your focus as situations change.	• You may not have access to the situations that need to be observed. • Your presence may cause changes in what you are trying to observe. • It may be difficult to observe enough situations to be able to make generalizations.
One-on-One Interviews	
• You can build relationships. • You can pick up messages through tone and nonverbal communication. • You can get individuals to clarify details.	• Gaining access to the people you need to interview may not be easy. • Telephone interviews sometimes catch people off guard and keep them from communicating. • Success relies heavily on good interviewing skills.
Focus Groups	
• You can get a lot of data in a short period of time. • You can take advantage of the ideas generated through brainstorming. • You can bring together people who otherwise might not communicate.	• Groups may be more difficult to schedule. • Individuals may censor themselves in front of other people. • The information you get may be irrelevant to your situation.
Surveys	
• You can get a lot of data, inexpensively, from many people. • You can get information from people who may otherwise be inaccessible. • Anonymous answers promote greater openness.	• You can't clarify questions people don't understand. • You can't identify the exact sources of the responses, so they may be difficult to interpret. • Convincing respondents of the survey's confidentiality may be difficult, so you may not get open and honest responses.

Caveat Emptor

Unfortunately, this is virtually impossible under the traditional ground rules of customer interaction. For millennia, business's attitude toward customers was summarized in the adage "caveat emptor" ("let the buyer beware"). Customers, responding in kind, adopted an equally detached view of their suppliers.

Under caveat emptor, communication between customer and supplier organizations is minimal. When the parties do interact, it is usually to negotiate price. The supplier's goal is to receive maximum return (most often monetary) on whatever product or service it provides. The customer, on the other hand, seeks to pay as little as is necessary to gain the benefits of the required product or service, even if driving a hard bargain also means driving the supplier out of business.

Under caveat emptor, the customer and supplier both seek *instant gratification.* They focus strictly on the short-term—making the most of *this* transaction.

Accommodation

In recent years, most business organizations have distanced themselves from the caveat emptor philosophy of customer relations. "Accommodative" customer-supplier relationships now appear to be the norm.

In the accommodative relationship, the customer and supplier organizations maintain separate and distinct goals, and their communications are still dedicated primarily to negotiation. But each is now cognizant of the other's interests. And each sees that it may be advantageous to yield, at times, to the interests of the other.

For example, the customer who desires reliable sources of raw materials (or other vital inputs) will be hesitant to make price demands that would drive a worthy supplier out of business. The supplier, in turn, sees that the value of predictable future demand can mitigate value lost through short-term price concessions. Both parties are therefore prepared to bend somewhat to the will of the other, and negotiations expand to cover issues beyond price and beyond the immediate transaction. The accommodative customer and supplier agree to defer some level of instant gratification in exchange for increased *stability* in the relationship.

CUSTOMER-SUPPLIER PARTNERSHIP

Today, a few business organizations are experimenting with a radically different form of customer interaction: the Customer-Supplier Partnership.

Partnering customer and supplier organizations behave as if they were one company (at least in the areas in which they've agreed to partner), helping to improve each other's work processes and sharing each other's successes and failures. Underlying the partners' interactions is a belief quite contrary to caveat emptor: For me to succeed, you must succeed.

Ironically, customer and supplier achieve this high level of trust, communication, and mutual understanding by shifting their focus *away* from each other to concentrate instead on a superordinate goal: Satisfy the ultimate customer.

Procter & Gamble and Wal-Mart, for example, are applying total quality concepts to reduce non-value-adding elements in their joint business systems and to maximize quality and value for their shared ultimate customers—the consumers who buy P&G products in Wal-Mart stores. The same principle also applies within organizations when separate departments or divisions work together to fulfill a superordinate mission.

Partnering customer and supplier organizations defer instant gratification and move beyond negotiation by focusing on a shared, superordinate goal. This, in turn, allows them to work as one to achieve *breakthroughs*. Having made their work processes as effective as possible on an independent basis, the customer and supplier combine their resources and know-how to seek quantum leaps that can be achieved only by working together.

IT'S LEGAL, AND YOUR SECRETS ARE SAFE

Before discussing when and how to pursue customer-supplier partnerships, we'll briefly address two concerns that almost always arise when we describe this approach.

The first concern is anti-trust laws. Let us assure you that we advocate only legal customer-supplier partnerships. Partnering generates competitive advantage through superior performance, not preferential treatment. By partnering, your organization may learn that efficient MIS systems are essential to your customers' success. You then make your own MIS systems more compatible with those used by your key customers. You have made it much easier and less costly to do business with your organization. And you have demonstrated your commitment to your customers' success.

Your competitors are free to follow suit. But will they? Few companies are willing to go to the extraordinary lengths required to partner with their customers. (In fact, ask yourself, would you scrap your entire MIS system and build a new one to get closer to your customers?) Partnering poses challenges that most businesses are either too complacent or too arrogant ("We're the best! We don't have to change for anybody!") to tackle.

The second concern most often raised about partnering involves trade secrets. Fortunately, you do not need to share trade secrets to partner with your customers and suppliers, as evidenced in the examples cited below. YOU ARE IN CONTROL of what you share. On the other hand, as in personal relationships, the more you can reveal of your ways of thinking and operating, the greater the potential benefits of the customer-supplier partnership.

WHEN TO PARTNER

We do not recommend the partnering approach for your every interaction with customers. It would be too time consuming. And, in many cases, it is simply impossible. An automobile manufacturer, for example, could not sit down face-to-face with every customer who might drive its new model mini-van. It could, however, partner with its dealer network. It might even gather a representative sample of parents to learn more about the demands of *their* customers—the children, pets, and other family members who rely on them for transportation.

In general, customer-supplier partnerships are best to apply between organizations or to close gaps between component parts within organizations. Partnering entails a significant investment of your time and energy, and should be implemented first with your most important customers and suppliers.

Here's a sampling of situations in which customer-supplier partnerships may prove especially productive.

• *When attempting to clarify customer needs and preferences.* You can't keep customers happy if you don't know what they want. And partnering is a great way to test your assumptions about what key customers really desire and expect from your organization.

For example, when Victor Rosansky facilitated a customer-supplier conference P&G had arranged with Wal-Mart, he asked executives from each company to describe what influences shoppers—the "ultimate customers" shared by both firms—to buy P&G products in Wal-Mart stores. Interestingly, P&G's marketing people operated on the assumption that shoppers look for special discounts. P&G therefore emphasized discounts and sales promotions, believing that the immediate customer, Wal-Mart, appreciated such efforts to move products off its shelves.

But it wasn't so. The Wal-Mart team stressed "low everyday prices" because they assumed that steady pricing is a big part of what motivates shoppers to choose one retail chain over another. Suddenly it was clear that the two organizations were pursuing contradictory strategies in their attempts to please their ultimate customers. The discounting prevalent in P&G's marketing strategy actually worked against Wal-Mart's emphasis on steady pricing.

Customer and supplier organizations generally form their own, independent perceptions of what ultimate customers need and prefer, then pursue separate strategies based on those independent perceptions. (Similarly, various departments and divisions within organizations tend to become functionally autonomous over time, pursuing disconnected and even conflicting missions.) Until these perceptions are merged, even an organization as experienced and savvy as Procter & Gamble can misread what an important customer truly wants and needs.

Rosansky then mixed the P&G and Wal-Mart executives together into small groups and put them to work shaping an accurate picture of the ultimate customer that both companies could share. From that point on, the conversations took on a decidedly different tone. The leaders of P&G and Wal-Mart now understood more about one another than ever before. What's more, they were now pursuing a common, superordinate goal: Satisfy the ultimate customer. As is so often the case, this increased understanding and sense of shared purpose led directly to increased levels of trust.

• *When seeking breakthroughs in cycle time and process efficiency.* Through vigilant analysis and continuous improvement of work processes, your own employees may be able to reduce work process variation down to two or three times its theoretical limits, after which they are likely to "hit the wall." The work processes simply cannot be improved further.

Or so it seems. When confronted with such an impasse, you should certainly consider stepping out of the confines of your own perspective to drink in the perspective of your customers. The P&G and Wal-Mart relationship also illustrates this point.

In a particularly frank (and constructive) exchange, a P&G executive first noted that the stocks of Pampers, Folger's coffee, Spic-and-Span, Crest, and Tide delivered on time to Wal-Mart often took days to actually appear on store shelves. "We've gone to a lot of trouble to make our delivery system the most reliable in the world," he said. "But what good does it do either of us if the product just sits on your loading dock?" The P&G executive pointed out that, "Every time we make a delivery, our drivers and your receivers go over the entire shipment to confirm that our truck contains the goods to be invoiced. It's a waste of time, for us and for you."

"We agree," replied the late Sam Walton, founder of Wal-Mart.

"Excuse me?" This was not the response the P&G team had expected.

"We agree with what you just said. Look, we must spend $3 million a month counting and confirming each and every delivery you make to our stores. So we *have* data. So do you. And I'll bet our data and your data would both tell us the same thing: Sometimes there's a little less on the trucks than it says on your invoice, sometimes there's a little more. But, over time, it all evens out." Everyone in the room seemed to concur with this assessment. "You make a good point," Walton concluded. "Checking your shipments is a waste of time and money. We'll stop doing it."

This triggered an exchange of glances on the P&G side of the table. "That's it? We give you an invoice and you just pay it, on trust?"

Walton shrugged. "We shouldn't trust you?" he asked.

P&G was, of course, quite worthy of Wal-Mart's trust. Thus,

the executives had surfaced an opportunity to eliminate a mountain of unnecessary administrative procedures that cost *both* companies millions of dollars each year and, so far as anyone could tell, did nothing to serve the ultimate customer. With that breakthrough, they went on to hammer out a practical framework for a new just-in-time inventory system—one that would keep Wal-Mart's shelves consistently stocked with P&G products and, at the same time, dramatically streamline shipping and receiving procedures.

In later months the customer-supplier dialogue was expanded down through the middle management ranks of both firms. Service levels as measured by both P&G and Wal-Mart improved significantly. The new just-in-time shipping procedures created a cash cushion for Wal-Mart (primarily by reducing financing costs). P&G's production cycle became significantly more predictable and cost effective. And Wal-Mart started buying so many P&G products that it is now the company's single largest customer.

• *When creating or modifying products and services.* The early discussions between P&G and Wal-Mart also highlighted the subtle ways in which partnering can eliminate much of the guesswork *and* risk that normally accompanies product development.

A P&G executive complained to someone at Wal-Mart: "Sometimes when we've developed product with your needs in mind, you've turned around and used it against us." The exec pointed to new packaging P&G once designed, in part, to take up less space on the store shelf, so retailers like Wal-Mart would not have to restock so frequently. But Wal-Mart used the extra shelf space to stock a competing product.

Someone on the Wal-Mart side remembered the incident and replied, "Think about what you're saying. You give us no clue about what you're doing or why you're doing it. Then you're surprised when we don't respond exactly as you expected. We can't guess what's in your heads." Other members of the Wal-Mart team nodded in silent agreement. "But you know, we *could* do a lot to help you improve your packaging," the Wal-Mart executive continued. "We know more than anybody about how shoppers scan shelves and what they look for in a package. Why don't you ever tap into us?"

It was a good question, and it triggered a series of similarly good questions. What began as a complaint about Wal-Mart's use of shelf space turned into a bountiful exchange of ideas for avoiding future misunderstandings and, more importantly, for how these two industry leaders could help each other become even more successful in serving the ultimate customer.

• *When managing cultural diversity.* In 1989, Federal Express asked Rosansky to lead a partnering conference for newly acquired shipping businesses that were now part of Federal Express in Europe. Most of the players gathered in Brussels had been direct competitors to one another before signing on with Federal Express. Past animosities and differences in their corporate cultures (not to mention centuries-old nationalistic rivalries) would make it challenging for this group to meld into an effective operating team.

Rosansky guessed that a traditional "let us reason together" approach would be ineffective in the face of such diversity. He chose instead to apply the principles of partnering. He asked the group to stop talking about one another (or, in the case of the French and the Italians, to stop *yelling* about one another), and to focus instead on the customers they all served. What did the customer want and need from them?

No, the disputes and differences of the past did not magically vanish into the air. But the group's focus did shift to the common ground. The participants were able to see that they were, and always had been, on the same side. Even as competitors each had tried foremost to serve the customer. Partnering principles enabled even this fractious group to see that—by combining their diverse experience, skills, and insights—they could serve customers even better together than they had on their own.

• *When headaches just won't go away.* Conflicts also develop in long-standing business relationships. And when those conflicts become headaches that just won't go away—despite the honest efforts of both parties to resolve the problem—the partnering structure can be the cure.

When P&G went through an especially bumpy stretch with one of its key suppliers, an advertising agency, it initiated a customer-supplier dialogue (including two sessions facilitated by Victor Rosansky). The participants in these discussions agreed to focus on their shared work process rather than on the individual practitioners involved.

Together, representatives of P&G and the agency analyzed the advertising development process and quickly concurred that ads are completed in three stages: strategy, creative, and implementation. The participants further agreed that in developing ads together, most of the headaches they experienced cropped up in the creative stage when the ad copy is written.

So the source of the problem must be somewhere in the creative stage, right? Wrong. After further analyzing the process, both parties realized that, while most objections arose in the creative stage, the *source* of the objections lay in the strategy stage.

The goal of the strategy stage is to arrive at a shared perception of the targeted consumers (the "ultimate customers" in this case) and then to achieve consensus on what the ad must communicate to positively influence these consumers' buying patterns. However, many developing ads were pushed into the creative phase too soon, before the strategy was well-defined. And without a clear strategic context the senior decision makers were all too likely to send even virtually finished ads, quite literally, back to the drawing board.

Once they identified the true source of the problem, P&G and the agency began redesigning the strategy phase of advertising development. Together they streamlined the process and removed much of the needless stress and rework from their customer-supplier relationship.

The examples cited above do not cover the full spectrum of situations in which it may be appropriate to pursue customer-supplier partnerships. If you take some time to explore such opportunities with your colleagues (and eventually with your customers), we feel certain you will unearth partnering opportunities we might never think to suggest.

In every customer-supplier partnership, however, your most fundamental goal is to build "barriers to entry" against your competitors. Partnering improves *relationships*. And a competitive edge in relationships is not easily matched. Through joint work process improvement, partnerships also enable you to reduce the *total cost of doing business* with your organization, so you can be the most cost-effective provider, even when your prices are significantly higher than those of your competitors. What's more, when your customers work with you to develop new products or to tailor your work processes specifically to meet their needs, they "have skin in the game." They've made *an investment in you*. And few customers will quickly or thoughtlessly abandon that investment.

HOW TO PARTNER

At the request of Federal Express, our colleague Rob Evans developed some basic "how to" guidelines, which he calls "The Five P's of Partnering":

1) Select the Right *P*artner
2) Select the Right *P*rocess
3) Select the Right *P*eople
4) Select the Right *P*itch
5) Select the Right *P*follow-through

Fortunately, the good folks at Federal Express appreciate Rob's sometimes unorthodox means of making a point. In fact, these "Five P's" have been widely distributed and applied throughout Federal Express, in both the U.S. and Europe. Let's more closely examine each "P":

• *The Right Partner.* Since partnering requires an investment of time and effort, be selective. Look for partners who are senior enough to override excuses and drive change; who share your desire or need for breakthroughs; and who have demonstrated a willingness to innovate and achieve win-win solutions.

• *The Right Process.* You can't work on everything at once. So give priority attention to work processes that provide maximum benefit to the ultimate customer; offer the greatest potential return on investment; are perceived as "important" by both parties; could create a competitive advantage for both customer and supplier; and could be improved within a reasonably short time frame.

• *The Right People.* To make the partnering initiative a success, you must bring together the right people to represent both the customer and supplier. By "the right people" we mean key decision makers (of roughly equal rank) from each organization; good listeners; people in a position to implement your ideas to improve processes; and creative, positive thinkers.

• *The Right Pitch.* When approaching potential partners, think about their "currencies" (What could a partnering experience provide that they might value?) and position your offer accordingly. Ask yourself, What will make partnering attractive? What data do you need to make this offer compelling? Who should be your first point of contact? What process improvement opportunities do you have in mind? How might successful process improvement benefit the ultimate customer shared by you and your potential partner?

• *The Right Pfollow-through.* The partnering meeting must conclude with an explicit plan. This plan should include the formation of quality action teams comprised of representatives from both organizations; a well-defined methodology for process improvement; clearly defined deliverables; specific measures of success; and a timetable for completion of your objectives.

The "Five P's" spell out the fundamental preconditions for a successful customer-supplier partnership. Now let's take a look at the partnering process itself. This figure outlines the primary tasks to be completed by the partnering customer and supplier.

The first order of business is to identify the ultimate customers shared by both parties (or to agree on a comparable superordinate goal). Though rarely difficult, this step is essential. You cannot be certain that everyone has the *same* ultimate customers in mind until such customers are explicitly named.

Next, you and your partner will explore the ultimate customer's needs and preferences. As related in our account of the P&G/Wal-

▪ THE PARTNERING PROCESS ▪

```
                    ┌─────────────────────┐
                    │ 1. Identify "ultimate│
                    │    customers."       │
                    └─────────────────────┘
┌─────────────────────┐              │
│ 7. Convert to        │              ▼
│    standard operating│      ┌─────────────────────┐
│    procedures.       │      │ 2. Explore ultimate  │
└─────────────────────┘      │    customer          │
                             │    requirements.     │
                             └─────────────────────┘
┌─────────────────────┐              │
│ 6. Monitor and       │              ▼
│    measure.          │      ┌─────────────────────┐
└─────────────────────┘      │ 3. Identify and      │
                             │    analyze gaps.     │
┌─────────────────────┐      └─────────────────────┘
│ 5. Pilot             │
│    innovations.      │      ┌─────────────────────┐
└─────────────────────┘      │ 4  Improve joint     │
                             │    processes.        │
                             └─────────────────────┘
```

Mart conference, this component of the customer-supplier exchange may prove especially enlightening, since significant differences in the partners' underlying assumptions almost always rise to the surface.

In fact, you should be prepared for someone in the room to challenge almost anything you might say. When they do, try not to be defensive. Partnering works because it puts everyone's pet theories (and sometimes even their basic beliefs) to the test. Do your colleagues, customers, and suppliers see things as you do?

Think of the experience as a way of cleaning house. You don't want to save *every* notion that's been rattling around in your attic.

Besides, holding your beliefs up to the clear, penetrating light of objectivity may prove liberating, as it did for P&G and Wal-Mart when they escaped the tiresome and expensive shipping and invoicing procedures, which until they engaged in a customer-supplier dialogue had seemed inevitable

Once you and your partner have sounded each other out on ultimate customer requirements, you can identify and analyze the gaps between what your ultimate customers want and what your combined work processes actually provide. "Backwardation" is a particularly effective approach for this sort of work process analysis. Through backwardation, you and your partner examine key work processes *backwards* from the point at which each key process touches the ultimate customer. With each step back into your organization, you stop and ask, "How is this part of the process geared to the ultimate customer's needs? How could it be modified to better serve the ultimate customer?"

Backwardation does several things. It gives you a clear picture of where you are now. It reinforces the fact that *all* parts of the work process affect ultimate customer satisfaction. And it subjects each part of the process to a consistent, rational test of customer focus. Backwardation usually turns up wasteful redundancies and procedures that are followed without good reason. It also opens up opportunities for innovation, since the whole idea is to question if the current process is performing as it should.

We were once given a lesson in the power of backwardation by one of our own firm's key suppliers, a printing company. We had reached an impasse with this printer over the plastic tab inserts that divide the various modules in our TQM training workbooks. The printer's price for the tab seemed high. He was also hedging on quality control, although he promised to "make every effort" to ensure that the tabs were acceptable.

Just as we were preparing to seek other bids on the job, the

The PRIDE checklist is an excellent tool for discovering the requirements of the ultimate customer.

The PRIDE Categories of Requirements

Dimensions	Ultimate Customer Requirements
Product or Service	What are the critical products and/or services to be provided? What are the critical specifications for these products and/or services?
Relationship	How should the supplier and the ultimate customer work together?
Integrity	How should the supplier follow up to make sure the ultimate customer's requirements are met?
Delivery	When and how should the product or service be delivered?
Expense	What will the ultimate customer contribute or pay in time, resources, or money to get what he or she wants and to help empower the supplier to meet the customer's requirements?

Step 1. Working on your own, describe your perspectives on what the ultimate customer requires in each of the five PRIDE dimensions. Then rank each requirement in order of its priority. (Your partner customer/supplier should also complete this step in advance of your meeting.)

Step 2. Together with your partner, merge your checklists and compare your rankings. Come to a consensus as to the ultimate customer's actual requirements and their relative importance.

Step 3. Meet with your ultimate customer to validate your perceptions.

printer requested a conference. We expected that he would again try to convince us that his price was fair. Instead, he asked questions about how we use the workbooks in the training workshops that we deliver to our customers. Why did we need the tabs?

We were put off by his question at first. After all, he had our specs. If we wanted tabs in our books, what business was that of his? But we answered him anyway, explaining that our trainers (and the client "facilitators" we certify to deliver our programs) often change the sequence of delivery to match the needs of particular groups or to suit their own personal preferences. The tabs allowed the workshop leader and the participants to jump around through the workbook, locating any particular section or page quickly and easily.

This interested our printer, triggering more questions from him. How did we set our workbook design standards? How did we define the requirements that determined those standards? How did we choose one design option over another? It dawned on us that the printer was doing just what we advocate to our clients. He was exploring one of our critical work processes (workbook design) *backwards* from the point of contact with the ultimate customer— the TQM workshop participant who uses *our* training materials printed by *his* company.

As we journeyed back through our design process with the printer, he offered suggestions: "Maybe color coding could serve the same function as the plastic inserts, and it would be cheaper," he ventured. "Yes," we replied, "but it doesn't look as sophisticated as the dividers." He pounced on the opportunity. "Perhaps I can help you find ways to use color coding that *do* look as sophisticated as the tabs. Or maybe we can come up with some other solution that would do all of that and more. Would you be willing to try?"

He had us. Of course we were willing to try. Over the rest of that conference and through several more discussions, we took our print supplier through our training process and our design process, explaining how we combine workbooks, video, and highly personalized instruction to teach TQM concepts and skills. Along the way we brainstormed options to make the materials work even better and harder for the ultimate customers we all share. Before long, we turned up several opportunities to make our workbooks even more user-friendly and aesthetically pleasing while cutting our production costs by 20 percent. Moreover, the new specs we developed together allowed our printer to guarantee higher levels of quality control and faster turn-around time, which enabled ODI to reduce its inventory of printed training materials.

To improve your work processes, both you and your partner must be ready and empowered to say yes to change. And that can be hard. Even in the face of irrefutable logic, we sometimes find it impossible to let go of the established and familiar. Think of Sam Walton abandoning the old receiving procedure and simply trusting that P&G's trucks contain what the invoices say they contain. Data and reason clearly indicated it was the right thing to do. But many less brave (and less senior) managers may have been incapable of crossing that line.

In most cases, though, we do recommend that you and your partner pilot your innovations within your respective organizations. As you move down from the management levels where most partnering discussions take place, employees may feel less empowered and more fearful of violating the status quo. You may therefore need to introduce innovations in baby steps, demonstrating to those who were not part of your partnering conference that management really does back these new ways of getting work done. Also, new approaches that *seemed* perfect during your face-to-face discussions may feel less compelling, and less practical, when you return to your everyday operations. So, as you pilot innovations,

Partnering Toolbox: Piloting Process Improvements

A pilot is usually the best way to test innovative improvements to your work processes. You can try out new ideas without getting bogged down by resistance or organizational red tape.

Guidelines for Piloting Process Improvements include:

- Test changes to your ongoing routines in small chunks or segments.

- View the pilot as an experiment in which to accumulate hard data. Don't expect your innovation to be a complete success right away.

- Do not overanalyze. (Don't fall victim to "analysis paralysis".)

- Select a site that has relatively low visibility.

- Involve people who are highly motivated to try something new.

- Get support from senior management to use the pilot as a means of gathering data and testing new methods for improving efficiency and increasing customer satisfaction.

you must keep the energy and spirit of the partnering exchange alive. Plan ongoing informal reviews of your progress. And be sure to keep sharing information and insights across both organizations. The initial customer-supplier conference between P&G and Wal-Mart, for example, ended with a commitment from both companies to pilot several ideas (including the just-in-time inventory system) to bring their shared work processes into alignment. Since then, P&G and Wal-Mart have dispatched numerous teams of managers and employees to study each other's work processes and to continue and expand the exchange of ideas on satisfying the ultimate customer.

You and your partner will also want to measure and monitor the effect of your innovations to make mid-course adjustments and, most significantly, to determine which new approaches were sufficiently successful to convert into standard operating procedures.

We'll wrap up our "How to" discussion with this important caution: *Not everyone can partner.* Partnering is intuitively sound. Therefore, one might assume that any organization can successfully pursue customer-supplier partnerships. But in truth, most organizations must adopt a fundamentally new set of attitudes and behaviors to partner effectively. It is especially futile to attempt partnering in a culture that is not committed to quality and customer satisfaction. The same is true for organizations whose leaders are not interested in change or committed to the pursuit of breakthrough. Under such conditions, you risk raising your customers' hopes and expectations, only to see them dashed by your organization's inability to respond to what customers want and need.

Sam Walton captured this truth best when we asked him if he objected to our sharing the "secrets" of partnering with others. He said, "I know most of my competitors. They're not ready to do this, no matter how well you explain it to them."

CONCLUSION

These days it seems like everyone talks about customer focus. We certainly do. Because the fact is you must know your customers to succeed in today's business environment. That much is clear to everyone.

And that is precisely why world-class leaders do not stop at knowing their *own* customers. To set their organizations apart, they expand the traditional definition of customer focus to include their *customers'* customers as well.

By focusing on a superordinate goal—satisfying the ultimate customer—you can achieve a profound understanding of your immediate customers' needs, aspirations, and beliefs. You can move well beyond the detached and distant customer-supplier exchanges that dominate most business relationships to form true partnerships with your customers, in which your interests and those of your customers become one and the same. The customer-supplier partnership is the most direct and powerful way to discover "opportunity gaps" that will dramatically enhance your competitive advantage.

In the next chapter we will shift our focus from your external customers to your employees to explore what you must do to effectively lead your people in total quality management.

6 ■ THE MAGIC INGREDIENT

DILBERT by Scott Adams

DILBERT reprinted by permission of UFS, INC.

Jerry Sparks used to hate going to work. And it wasn't the foul odors inside the Texaco refinery in Port Arthur, Texas, that bothered him. "My father and my grandfather both worked here," he says. "I knew what the place smelled like when I took the job. If you're going to work in a refinery, you'd better get used to it." Sparks could take the heat, too, even when it climbed up to 110 degrees. "Of course you get a lot of heat, but so does the guy out digging a ditch somewhere." No, Sparks never wasted time complaining about the smells, the weather, or anything else that nobody could change. What would be the use?

One thing *did* get under Sparks's skin, though—management. "The bosses would say, 'Do it this way 'cause this is how we're telling you to do it. We don't pay you to think. We pay you to work,'" Sparks recalls. "I think a lot of it was they were afraid we might know more than them," he adds, shaking his head at the memory.

As vice president of Oil, Chemical, and Atomic Workers Union

Local 4-23, Sparks may be more sensitive than most to how this made the refinery workers feel. "Remember, we're talking about full grown men, community leaders who coach little league teams, organize local fire departments . . . Hell, some of them were mayors of their towns," Sparks notes. "But once they punched in at the plant, they were expected to just shut up and do what the boss said, even when it made no sense at all. I put a lot of equipment together wrong just because that was how the boss told me to do it."

Understandably, Sparks did not relish the dawning of each new work day. But the worst part was, he could soon have no job at all.

By 1984, the refinery at Port Arthur (erected in 1903 by the upstart Texas Oil Company) was among the worst performers in the Texaco system, lagging far behind in productivity, profitability, and most other measures. Most of its equipment was installed prior to World War II. Major customers routinely rejected and returned its products. And management had just announced a layoff of more than one third of the plant's 4,000 employees. The Port Arthur plant was dying.

Into this troubled scenario strode Lee Townsend, the man who would turn Port Arthur around. The new plant manager was a tall, lean, greying executive with the bearing of an Air Force general. Townsend had worked his way up from a job not too different from the one Jerry Sparks was now in danger of losing. So the new boss understood how the people of Port Arthur were feeling.

"The employees had just seen the payroll of the refinery cut in half," Townsend says. "Friends who once worked by their side were gone. And those who were still there wondered 'Is this plant going to be here in five years? Will there be a job for me?' Very reasonable questions, under the circumstances."

Sparks, one of those posing the questions, was surprised but heartened by Townsend's reply. "He'd say this was *our* plant, and we could make it run good or we could shut it down," he recalls. "We weren't used to management saying things like that. Before too long," Sparks adds, "Townsend knew just about everybody by their first name. We'd never been nothing but a badge number before."

For Port Arthur's managers and supervisors, Townsend had several new job requirements: "Ask your employees their opinion, solicit their input, show respect, and give recognition for a job well done." He gave Port Arthur's supervisors just two options: Learn to listen to The Voice of the Employee or leave. "I made it clear that it would be my head on the platter, not theirs," Townsend notes. "If my way of doing things didn't work out, I'd take the blame. So nobody had an excuse not to give it a chance." Only a handful of his 220 supervisors departed.

Adamant as he was, Townsend understood that it would not be easy for his managers and supervisors to meet his demands. "The authoritarian management style had been the norm around here for many years," he explains. "So naturally, moving toward a more participative management approach caused a lot of stress and concern."

Townsend hired ODI specifically to help his supervisors make the required transition. A condensed version of the training we provided to management was offered to the refinery's production workers and craftsmen, so they would understand how and why they would be managed differently.

Townsend also rewrote the rules under which Port Arthur interacted with its customers—primarily other divisions of Texaco. The refinery had always interacted with its customers through Texaco's transportation department. When a customer rejected a shipment, Port Arthur would get a call from Transportation saying that a full tanker was on its way back to them. Refinery managers might then swear about the customer being so damned picky. But they couldn't ask customers *why* a shipment had been rejected, what they might do to set things right, or how to prevent it from happening again.

Townsend put his people in direct contact with The Voice of the Customer by sending them out of Port Arthur to visit the various Texaco divisions that bought their gasoline, fuel oil, jet fuel, lubricating oils, and chemical feedstock. Port Arthur personnel also established direct contact with the folks from the state of Texas who bought the plant's asphalt.

By 1986, a number of specific quality improvement initiatives were underway. "We looked for opportunities to start quality action teams, mostly within natural work groups on a voluntary basis," Townsend says. Managers and others who volunteered to lead problem-solving teams received two days of skills training.

Once Port Arthur employees learned to analyze and improve their work processes, successes came quickly. For example, one team dramatically reduced the time required to sample and test petroleum product after it has been loaded into tanker ships, thereby cutting demurrage (the cost of detaining a ship at the refinery beyond its scheduled stay) by an estimated $500,000 to $1 million per year and speeding product delivery to customers. Another team developed new procedures for eliminating back pressure in one of the plant's main power generators. This eliminated the need for new piping that would have cost several hundred thousand dollars.

As supervisors grew more adept at listening to and empowering their employees, as people throughout the refinery gained meaningful access to The Voice of the Customer, and as quality action team successes mounted, Townsend's prescription for Port Arthur began to look like a miracle cure. The same customers who routinely rejected Port Arthur products in the old days now consistently rate the plant's output as "excellent." Losses due to accidents are down 84 percent. Employee grievances have fallen by 65 percent. And, in a recent employee survey, 75 percent of employees agreed that working conditions have truly improved in the plant.

Perhaps most significant to Jerry Sparks is that the plant survived. Today, Port Arthur has returned to healthy profitability and is a valued and viable component of Star Enterprise, the joint venture formed in 1989 by Texaco Refining and Marketing East Inc. and Saudi Refining, Inc.

The Port Arthur story is one of our favorites because it shows what a remarkable difference an effective leader can make in an organization. True, we've described Lee Townsend in more heroic terms than he himself would use. But however we might tell the tale, the facts are clear. Before Townsend arrived on the scene, the Texaco refinery at Port Arthur was dying. Under his leadership, the refinery not only survived, it thrived.

In any organization, leadership is the "magic ingredient" that makes quality work. TQM is the headlong pursuit of a better future. No organization closes its rework gap or opens a significant quality advantage by conducting business as usual. Sooner or later, someone must step forward and lead the charge.

So naturally, this book offers plenty of advice on leadership. The problem is, "good" leadership is mostly a matter of behaving appropriately in your situation, your environment, and (most of all) to your followers. You therefore embrace "standard" leadership formulas at your peril.

THE NATURE OF TQM

With that caution in mind, let's frame our discussion of leadership within the one constant available to us: TQM itself. Unlike Management by Objectives, Zero Defects, or most other management concepts, TQM is *value* driven. And the core value of TQM is absolute focus on the customer. This, in turn, compels everyone to view your organization *horizontally*. That is, TQM demands that you balance your emphasis on departments and functions with an even greater understanding of, and focus on, the key work processes that cut across functions. Why? Because no one function in your organization can satisfy your customers. The success of that relationship depends on the sum total of everyone's efforts. Your organization's various functions must become like customers and suppliers to one another. By first meeting one another's needs, they can work together to improve horizontal work processes for the benefit of your organization's external customers.

Just as important, under TQM financial results like profit and cost-containment become *dependent* variables. TQM demands a "leap of faith": Focus on your customers, and the numbers on your bottom-line will surely grow.

THINKING STYLES

What kind of leadership is appropriate for a business organization that is value driven, believes that high performing, horizontal work processes are the key to its success, and pays more attention to its customers than to its profit reports?

To describe the leadership behaviors that are most appropriate to TQM, we often borrow from the Brain Dominance Model developed by our good friend Ned Herrmann, a researcher in creativity and learning.[1]

The Herrmann Brain Dominance Model is a metaphorical interpretation of how people think and learn. It contains four distinct thinking styles: those incorporating the left and right hemispheres as well as those incorporating the upper (cerebral) and lower (limbic) parts of the brain.

The upper left quadrant can be thought of as including analytical, mathematical, technical, and problem-solving qualities. The lower left is controlled, conservative, planned, organized, and administrative in nature. The lower right represents the interper-

Herrmann Brain Dominance Model

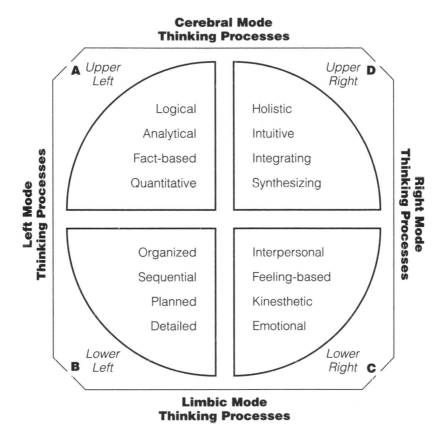

© 1986, Ned Herrmann

sonal, emotional, musical, and spiritual thinking modes. And the upper right contains the imaginative, synthesizing, artistic, holistic, and conceptual modes.

"No one style of thinking is better than the others," Ned stresses. "You are most effective when you optimize your ability to use all these types of thinking, depending on the need and the situation."

This is certainly true of the TQM leader. TQM is, after all, a fact-based management process. It requires everyone to analyze, understand, and continuously improve their own work processes. Further, your implementation of TQM must be meticulously planned and highly organized. It is up to you (and other leaders) to provide a clear, logical structure through which your employees can produce tangible, quantifiable quality improvements.

Yet you can hardly afford to overlook the right-mode needs of your people. If you fail to help your followers connect to TQM on some value-driven or emotional level, and if you fail to convey a "big picture" concept of what your organization is trying to accomplish through TQM, it's likely they will never use the TQM skills, structure, and metrics you provide.

You can see, then, that TQM leadership is a tall order, requiring command of all the thinking styles described in Ned Herrmann's interpretation of the Whole Brain Model. In this chapter, we will concentrate primarily on the right-mode side of the TQM leadership equation. That is, we will describe behaviors that are appropriate for creating a sense of urgency about quality improvement, for establishing and sustaining momentum in the TQM process, and for igniting a passion for satisfying your customers. In the next chapter, we will explain how to apply these inspirational leadership behaviors within a sequenced and highly structured left-mode approach for achieving customer-focused breakthrough.

WINNING HEARTS AND MINDS

We often say that the most important thing TQM leaders do is "win the hearts and minds of their people." And we place special emphasis on winning hearts. Once your people find a place in their hearts for TQM, once they care about it as much as you do, then their minds will surely follow. Here are nine specific leadership actions we feel are vital to gain your people's full and sincere commitment to TQM.

Get smart about quality. This is the very first piece of advice we give to anyone who wants to lead a TQM effort. You simply cannot be a credible champion of total quality management without first *understanding* total quality management.

Read books. Among those we recommend are *Kaizen, The Goal, Thriving on Chaos, Managing on the Edge, The Art of War, Quality Is Free,* and *Total Quality Control.* (A list of recommended TQM readings is provided in Appendix F.)

Your senior managers should also visit winners of the Malcolm Baldrige National Quality Award in the United States and of the Deming Prize in Japan. Virtually all prizewinning companies offer regularly conducted sessions sharing their TQM approaches and successes. (Appendix B includes lists of companies that have won the Baldrige Award or Deming Prize.)

Stress TQM's values first. Plenty of managers make speeches trying to rally the troops around goals such as "a three percent reduction in our cost of sale." But such pleas invariably fail because no matter how passionately you advocate them, certain objectives just are not meaningful to the average employee. We suggest that you explicitly connect TQM to issues your people *do* care about. That is, stress the values of TQM.

TQM offers something to everyone—the customer, the employee, and the business. And it stands for what most employees especially believe in—doing a job right the first time, being "the best" at what they do, and having everyone's ideas treated with respect. TQM values can (and should) serve as the common ground where everyone in your organization stands.

This was really the key to Lee Townsend's success at Port Arthur. Sure, everyone shared an interest in the plant's survival before he came. The problem was they shared no common ground short of survival. Everyone saw the raft going over the falls, and *still* they couldn't pull together on the same oar.

Townsend saved Port Arthur by aligning his most vital business objective (increasing the efficiency of the plant's work processes) with employee values (workers wanting more say in how they did their jobs). Through TQM, Townsend gave employees the power, opportunity, and skills to change how they completed their work. In return, they willingly participated in quality teams, improved the plant's efficiency and profitability, and dramatically increased customer satisfaction.

Define "The Right Things" to do. As a manager you set day-to-day priorities, assign tasks, and determine how employees will spend their time. But as a TQM leader, you must also work with your people to develop a vision defining The Right Things to do.

How You Do It

	Right Things Wrong	Right Things Right	
	Stress Improved Execution	**Stress Continuous Improvement**	What You Do
	Wrong Things Wrong	Wrong Things Right	
	Zero-base	**Clarify Goals**	

We recommend that managers throughout your organization regularly conduct The Personal Quality Audit (introduced in Chapter Four) with their work groups. In terms of a central task or vital work process, where do you and your people operate? Do you always do the Right Things Right or do you sometimes slide into one of the other three quadrants? Each situation implies a clear emphasis on what are The Right Things for you and your people to focus on, whether it's "zero-basing" a badly flawed work process or continuously improving a process that is already performing well.

No matter what approach you use, the important thing is to help employees understand their work in the context of customer requirements. When you set priorities and assign tasks, make sure your people understand the "why" as well as the "what" of your decisions.

Spread hope. "I believe the leader's ultimate job is to spread hope," Bob Galvin once told George Labovitz.

What the Motorola chairman captured in those few words is enormously important. Day after day, we see managers severely underestimate what their people can do. They fail to challenge their organization's perceived limits and, as a result, condemn their employees to perform at levels considerably below their true potential.

Galvin points to his company to illustrate this point. In the early 1980s, Japanese customers complained that Motorola's paging system did not meet their standards for quality. Motorola's engineers cried foul, insisting that the standards the Japanese proposed were technically impossible. But when Motorola executives voiced this protest, their Japanese customers simply wheeled out three Japanese-made pagers that already met the standards.

Motorola's leaders were confronted with a vivid truth: The quality standards their Japanese customers demanded were not only attainable but essential. If Motorola could not match this "impossible" level of quality performance, it would be driven out of the paging business.

Many other U.S. electronics firms challenged by comparable harsh realities folded their tents and conceded their markets to the Japanese. But Galvin and his executive colleagues at Motorola chose instead to "spread hope." They set out to convince their people that Motorola could perform at levels higher (*much* higher) than seemed possible at the time. And they implemented a remarkably intensive total quality management effort that focused the company first on meeting—and eventually on surpassing—the quality standards its engineers had once thought beyond their reach. The new technology Motorola developed in pursuit of its quality breakthrough also became the basis for its enormously successful new portable phones, which boast a projected reliable work-life of one hundred years. Spreading hope certainly worked for Bob Galvin and company.

Demand short-term results. You may have heard the TQM axiom "Quality is a journey, not a destination." It means that TQM is a commitment to long-term, continuous improvement, not a "quick-fix." And we couldn't agree more.

But in the real world people aren't very patient. They find it difficult to work hard at something when they're told the results won't be visible for months or even years. That's why we advise our clients to demand short-term results from their long-term TQM process.

We advocate what we call the "Quick-Start" approach. While you conduct customer research, train employees in quality skills, and lay the other foundations of TQM, turn loose a few hand-picked quality action teams on your most urgent quality issues or process improvement opportunities. (Just be certain your Quick-

Start teams are led by someone experienced and qualified in quality improvement.)

For example, Grumman Corporation used ODI-led Quick-Start teams to model the team problem-solving and process-improvement method now used throughout its operations. The Grumman Quick-Start teams

•saved $30 million in aircraft production costs by eliminating rework and scrap.

•reduced cycle time required to produce detail parts from 108 days to just 41 days.

•revamped an inventory system to save more than $2 million annually while significantly increasing on-time delivery to customers.

The subsequent vitality of total quality in Grumman brings to mind another axiom, one that dates back even before TQM: "Success breeds success."

Put your body into the process. Leading TQM is hard work, as Hybritech chairman Don Grimm can attest. Shortly after taking charge of the San Diego–based biotechnology firm in 1988 (it was acquired by Eli Lilly & Company in 1987), Grimm resolved to lead Hybritech in a new direction, one defined by total quality management. "Making the mental commitment to TQM was easy," he says. "Let's face it, a lot of executives think quality is good and they say so."

The next level of commitment, Grimm says, comes "when you really *believe* in the changes you're trying to make, when you've moved beyond the mental commitment to a spiritual commitment. At that point, questions about quality and customer satisfaction start driving every decision you make. It's not something you have to stop and think about. It's just the way you feel.

4   **Lead**

- Commit yourself to becoming a champion of TQM.
- Insist on the use of TQM to achieve organizational goals.
- Hold people accountable for supporting quality goals.
- Never compromise quality for schedule, volume, or cost.
- Ensure that TQM is part of decision making in all organizational and clinical processes.

3   **Manage**

- Chair a quality council, head a quality improvement team, and remove barriers.
- Establish TQM measures to track your organization's success.
- Implement an innovative rewards and recognition system for TQM efforts.
- Model doing Right Things Right.

2   **Support**

- Delegate the responsibility for TQM initiatives.
- Create senior management TQM initiatives.
- Kick off TQM training sessions for your people.
- Endorse TQM as a priority for the organization.
- Include TQM topics in presentations.

1   **Allow**

- Allow people in your organization to attend TQM training.
- Attend TQM training yourself.
- Create a TQM coordinator position that reports to senior management.
- Fund limited TQM training without becoming directly involved.
- Fund an exploratory TQM pilot effort.

For senior managers, TQM leadership is a function of their commitment. Many will "allow" or even "support" TQM. But only a handful will make the commitment required to "manage" and "lead" TQM.

"But the really decisive variable is the physical commitment," Grimm insists. "Employees can't look into your heart to see if you believe in what you're saying about quality. But they can and undoubtedly will make judgments based on your actions. They're watching to see if you will put your body into the process. Will you sit in the TQM training sessions, just like everyone else? Will you serve on quality action teams? Will *you* change, or are you just demanding that they change?"

Don Grimm changed. His actions backed his demand that everyone fully participate in TQM. "I was always pushing people to get involved," he recalls. "I'd tell them, 'I'm here doing it. You should be, too.' "

Grimm says he is now "doing things that are very different from what I used to do as the big cheese." He spends about one-third of his time on receiving training, talking to employees about quality, participating in problem-solving teams, visiting customers, and visiting other companies to understand how they improved quality.

Grimm's hard work has paid handsome dividends. Virtually everyone at Hybritech is now actively involved in the total quality process, cutting downtime in key manufacturing processes by as much as 50 percent, improving accuracy and consistency across research, development, and manufacturing functions, and achieving positive service ratings from more than 90 percent of Hybritech's customers. Not coincidentally, Hybritech also tripled its sales revenues and significantly increased its profitability.

Work for your people. Make no mistake about it, Fred Smith is the boss at Federal Express. But the CEO doesn't spend a lot of time pressing employees to meet his needs. Instead, he defines his job as meeting *their* needs.

"Here's the message we try to communicate to our people: The purpose of a business is to gain and keep customers. A courier's job, for example, is to work directly for the customer. A front-line manager's job is to make the courier's job easier, and her manager's job is to make the front-line manager's job easier, and so on until you get to the executive suite, where the job is to do whatever it takes to help everybody do their best. If you look at your organization chart this way, everyone in the company is the CEO's customer," Smith says.[2]

Bob Loughead, former president of Weirton Steel in West Virginia, was a leader cut from the same cloth as Fred Smith. Loughead spent his first few days on the job walking around his company asking employees, "What's getting in the way of us making the best steel in the world?" He then wrote down each employee's reply on his pad of paper. After talking to hundreds of people throughout the company, Loughead held the pad high above his head and declared, "OK, now I've got my job description."

Lead with passion. If there's one thing great TQM leaders all share in common, it's passion. Fred Smith, Don Grimm, Lee Townsend, Bob Galvin, and Roger Milliken are all dogged and impatient champions of TQM. They convey an unbridled sense of urgency, *demanding* that their people get involved in efforts to improve quality and increase customer satisfaction. And if they "go ballistic," it probably won't be over a trifling policy violation or someone's failure to meet a quota. It will be because an employee knowingly let a customer down, because a manager "shut down" employee input, or because someone, somewhere transgressed against the values that they, and their organizations, stand for.

Lead with compassion. But if great TQM leaders lead with passion, they also lead with *compassion.* They balance their insistence that everyone get involved in TQM with "permission to fail," for failure will surely be part of any grand experiment. They are also in the habit of asking "Why?" (not "Who?") when things go wrong. They search out the process or systematic causes of problems instead of trying to pin blame on an individual. Finally, they are acutely aware of their people's emotional needs, and of how these needs change with the introduction of a TQM process.

Willi Railo, our ODI colleague in Norway and the author of several works on leadership, stresses "Each and every employee has a 'security zone' in which he or she is capable of taking effective action. When you make demands that require people to move outside of this zone, they may be emotionally incapable of following your lead."

Therefore, when pressing for fundamental change or dramatic improvements (such as those typically sought under TQM), you must make special efforts to expand your followers' security zones. "Otherwise, your employees may not follow you, even if you do everything else right," Willi notes. "Basic things make all the difference," he adds. "Firm schedules, for example, help reduce people's fear of change. Don't just say what you want. Specify *when* you want it. Clear, simple, consistent signals tend to enhance security. Ambiguous, complex, inconsistent signals diminish it.

"As a leader, it's your job to simplify matters in any way you can," Willi concludes. "Don't leave the path toward your goals cluttered with obstacles. And remember, nearly everyone is less secure than they appear."

CONCLUSION

These are among the "make or break" behaviors to win your people's hearts and minds over to TQM. In organizations where TQM succeeds and endures, leaders almost always do these things. And in organizations where people fail to embrace TQM, it is almost always because the leaders did not fulfill one or more of these obligations. Leadership really is the magic ingredient in making quality work.

The burden of TQM leadership falls as heavily on the middle manager as on the CEO. Ask employees within most large organizations to identify "senior management" and they'll almost always point to managers somewhere near the middle of the corporate hierarchy. Employees perceive middle managers as having the most immediate, visible, and meaningful influence on their work lives. (What do you imagine Jerry Sparks would have thought if the chairman of Texaco had announced his commitment to TQM, but Lee Townsend advocated business as usual?) Employees believe in the chain of command. They know that what the CEO says is important, but they study their immediate managers and supervisors to interpret what is "real" and what is "just talk." Therefore, if your middle managers leave the business of quality leadership solely to your executives, TQM will never be "real" in the minds of most of your people.

NOTES

1. Ned Herrmann's model incorporates the research of Roger Sperry and Paul MacLean. For details see Ned Herrmann, *The Creative Brain* (Lake Lure, N.C.: Brain Books, 1988).

2. "Blueprints for Service Quality: The Federal Express Approach," 1991, AMA Membership Publications Division, New York, NY 10020.

7 ■ LEADING CUSTOMER-FOCUSED BREAKTHROUGH

DILBERT by Scott Adams

DILBERT reprinted by permission of UFS, INC.

We often tell the story about a young boy who gets lost at Coney Island. Reluctantly, a veteran police officer comes to the child's aid, taking his hand and leading him through the crowds in search of his missing parents. The cop's worst expectations are soon realized as the boy grows increasingly disconsolate, whiny, and obnoxious. When the pair settles on a bench for a brief rest, the boy sobs, "Do you think (sniff) we'll ever (sniff) find my parents?" The cop shakes his head wearily and replies, "I don't know, kid. There must be a thousand places where they could be hiding."

Many business leaders who commit their organizations to TQM are just like that kid's parents. "TQM will be exciting!" the executives say. "It will be fun to do! Let's get on with it!" So their people jump into the process, confident that their leaders will guide them through the unknown. But one day, employees and middle managers look up and realize that the senior managers are all gone! They've disappeared from the TQM scene, leaving their followers lost and alone in strange territory. "Where'd they go?" the employees ask as they search frantically for the executives. Of course, there are a thousand places where senior managers could be hiding....

In the preceding chapter, we suggested that leadership—beginning with senior management and extending down through the middle management ranks—is "the magic ingredient" for making quality work. But even a magic ingredient is of little value if it won't stay in the mix.

Why do senior managers drift away from TQM? In most cases, executives lose interest because *total quality management never became critical to running the business.* When TQM remains an "extra," senior managers inevitably tire of their TQM leadership burdens. They quietly slip free of their stated or implied commitment to serve as quality champions and shift their focus back to their traditional roles as business strategists and functional managers.

Ironically, world-class leaders realize that *you can't shape strategy or run your business without TQM.* They know that, until you are "hard wired" to your customers, your business objectives are little more than elaborate guesswork. Similarly, you can't gauge your company's potential or consistently influence its inner workings until you've tapped into the voices of your employees and work processes.

A fundamental step toward making quality work, then, is making TQM leadership *the same as* "running the business." This, in a nutshell, is what *hoshin kanri* is all about.

HOSHIN

Say "hoshin" to the average Western manager, and he or she might very well reply "Gesundheit." That's because *hoshin kanri* has been most widely applied (and was perfected) in Japan. Still, like much of the Japanese version of TQM, *hoshin* is basically an adaptation of Western strategic planning concepts and can be very effectively applied in the Western business culture.

The word *hoshin* means "policy." *Kanri* means "management." Therefore, the literal translation of *hoshin kanri* is "policy management." This hardly does justice to the dynamic power of the approach, however, so we often refer to *hoshin* as Breakthrough Leadership.

The basic elements of Breakthrough Leadership are 1) planning, 2) deployment, and 3) review. Of course, *all* business leaders set plans, deploy plans, and then review the outcomes. So what's different about Breakthrough Leadership? Let's consider each of the three basic elements in sequence.

Breakthrough Leadership

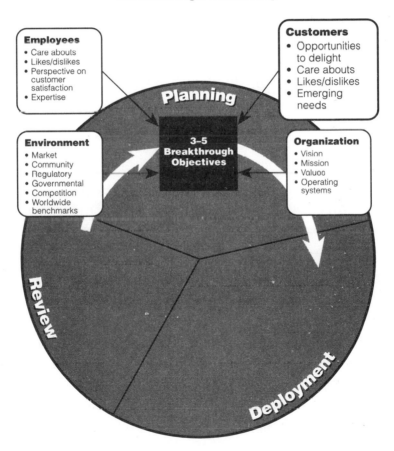

1 ▪ PLANNING FOR BREAKTHROUGH

Some aspects of *hoshin*-style planning will be familiar to most readers. For example, Breakthrough Leadership calls on the organization to articulate a clear Vision (Where are we going?), a Mission (What do we do?), and Values (What do we stand for?). Most major business organizations today have at least attempted to address these issues.

However, planning in the *hoshin* context is not at all like the annual business and strategic planning processes familiar to most executives and managers. Most Western business plans are driven almost solely by financial and budgetary considerations, while *hoshin*-style planning places extraordinary emphasis on customer-focused breakthrough.

The end product of *hoshin*-style planning is a set of three (no more than five) clearly defined breakthrough objectives. The number of targeted breakthroughs is explicitly limited to safeguard against all organizations' universal tendency to pursue too many objectives at once.

Each objective is to be achieved by your organization over a three- to five-year period. However, dramatic signs of progress toward the targeted breakthroughs are expected much sooner than that and specific interim objectives are articulated every year. For example, if the five-year objective in a factory is to "reduce facility downtime to zero," the first-year *hoshin* (literal translation "policy" or "directive") could be "train all line workers in the art and technology of both repair and preventive maintenance"; the second-year *hoshin* "design and produce our own replacement parts" (eliminate the need to order replacement parts from outside sources); the third year "assume responsibility for design of all new facilities" (to ensure that zero downtime is designed at concept stage); and so on, until the objective is fulfilled. Naturally, as objectives are realized, they are replaced with new critical priorities for the subsequent period.

Just as significantly, each of your breakthrough objectives should require the organization to "stretch" to do much more than your people currently think they are capable of doing. *Hoshin* is based on the premise that the "impossible" (that is, the seemingly unattainable breakthrough) often *becomes* possible once it has been captured in a goal, assuming that the goal is suitably compelling and fully supported by the organization's leaders.

CULTIVATING CONSENSUS

This is not to say, however, that leaders can simply dictate "pie-in-the-sky" breakthrough objectives, then sit back and watch their people struggle to fulfill them. Quite the opposite is true. Most employees simply will not extend themselves in pursuit of objectives they do not value.

Hoshin-style planning works because it requires leaders to achieve extraordinarily high levels of consensus. Virtually everyone in the organization (The Voice of the Employee) must agree that the breakthrough objectives chosen are worth pursuing. Contrast this to traditional planning approaches that make strategic analysis and decision making the exclusive domain of senior managers (abetted by small staffs of "experts") and again you see that planning under Breakthrough Leadership is a horse of a very different color.

Some observers have suggested that consensus (or lack thereof) is a key distinction between the "typical" Japanese work culture and the work culture found in most Western business organizations. Some have further theorized that the Japanese, a relatively homogenous people in racial and sociocultural terms, have gained a competitive advantage in part because they are by nature and by conditioning inclined toward consensus, while the more diverse composition of Western peoples (not to mention the high value we place on individual freedoms) predisposes North American and European workers to "go their own way."

Perhaps. But there may be a simpler explanation. The leaders of the best Japanese firms continuously and laboriously seek consensus in planning. They truly believe consensus is a prerequisite to achieving their goals. Therefore, if the Japanese work culture exudes consensus, it may be because Japanese managers work so hard to *cultivate* consensus.

The experience of a growing number of U.S. firms indicates that American workers are very much the same as their Japanese counterparts in at least one regard: They tend to support what they help create. For example, Zytech, Inc., a winner of the 1991 Malcolm Baldrige Award,[1] involves large numbers of its employees from the janitors to the chief financial officer in its planning process. Even some larger firms are now cultivating consensus through widespread involvement in planning. Throughout most of Hewlett-Packard, middle managers are now active partners in setting the company's guiding plans and goals.

How does one involve hundreds and even thousands of people in creating three to five concisely-worded breakthrough objectives? Proven consensus building tools, such as the Affinity Diagram and Catchball, are vital.

As groups throughout your organization develop Affinity Diagrams, consistent themes and priorities will emerge. Senior management should first summarize these major themes for your people, then apply the Affinity Diagram once more to prioritize the best of the ideas and insights offered. The most compelling of these should become the substance of your organization's breakthrough objectives.

Catchball, when properly played, is a freewheeling exercise in which your organization's strategic priorities and your people's ideas for achieving those vital objectives pass rapidly down the hierarchical ladder, across functions, and then back up the chain of

Hoshin Toolbox: The Affinity Diagram

The Affinity Diagram is an excellent tool for dealing with complex (and potentially chaotic) challenges, such as organization-wide planning. Convened in small groups, your managers and/or employees use the Affinity Diagram to develop and propose new organizational goals and to suggest specific actions or projects designed to bring about targeted change.

Each group completes the Affinity Diagram in eight steps:

- Select a theme, issue, or a critical question based on insights gained from customers or in response to senior management's request for input.

- In groups of five to ten people, discuss the selected theme and draft questions to be used to generate ideas about the theme.

- Using one-line statements, brainstorm ideas and commit them to Post-it notes.

- Place the Post-its on a flip chart.

- Move the Post-its around on the flip chart, putting the individual ideas into groups. Don't force relations among the Post-its. Group the ideas according to their clear and natural "affinity" to one another.

- Write one-line labels or summaries capturing the essence of each group of Post-its. These should be spontaneous statements containing an action verb.

- Further consolidate the groups until no more than three to seven groups remain.

- Capture the group headlines and components on paper to share and discuss with others, including senior management.

command. Your breakthrough objectives and plans are thus enriched by the insights and input of hundreds of "players." And, by providing opportunities for everyone to help shape your organization's future, you cultivate consensus and motivate employees to take action in the targeted areas.

Of course, the single most important factor in shaping your breakthrough objectives is The Voice of the Customer. Partnering

Japanese business leaders (many of whom share Americans' love for baseball) have developed a powerful technique for soliciting employee input and cultivating consensus. They call this technique "catchball". Senior managers circulate throughout the organization engaging middle managers and employees in "games" of catchball. The rules of the game are simple.

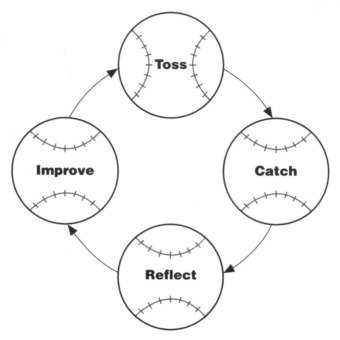

First comes the "toss"—someone throws out an idea for consideration. In the planning phase, for example, senior managers will often toss out potential breakthrough objectives for reactions from their employees. Later on, in the deployment phase, the leader will go around asking employees to offer ideas on how the organization might achieve the targeted breakthroughs.

Once an idea has been tossed, everyone else present must "catch" it (that is, understand it) and "reflect" on it. This isn't as simple as it sounds. Like a child learning to secure a ball firmly in the glove before reaching in to return the throw, most managers and employees (and executives for that matter) must concentrate to give an idea fair consideration before reacting. Then, anyone with a suggestion for how to "improve" or build upon the first idea offered—as opposed to offering a completely different idea, thereby undermining the first—can make the next "toss" in the form of an enhanced iteration of the original idea. Others then catch, reflect upon, and further improve it. This catchball cycle is repeated until an idea is either fully developed or abandoned.

(described in Chapter Five) is but one of many ways to gain extraordinary insight into customers' stated and unstated needs. We also recommend frequent executive-level visits to key customer sites, middle management and employee exchanges to study customers' work processes, a rigorous program of customer surveys, prevention-oriented customer complaint handling systems, and continuous informal gathering of customer data by everyone in the organization. The reader may also wish to review the literature on Quality Function Deployment, a well-defined, cross-functional TQM method now being applied with success in a number of industries. Any and all of these approaches may be valuable to tap into The Voice of the Customer, so long as they are applied in the true spirit of customer-supplier partnership: "For me to succeed, you must succeed."

Other significant influences in shaping the breakthrough plan include the capabilities and potential of your key operating systems and the ever-shifting realities of the outside environment, including worldwide benchmarks.

BENCHMARKING

Any discussion of *hoshin*-style planning must include benchmarking, the study of other organizations that demonstrate excellence and extraordinary performance in areas relevant to your company. In fact, benchmarking is one of the most popular activities to stem from the total quality movement.

However, we cannot vouch for the effectiveness of all the benchmarking activities now underway. Many organizations mistakenly attempt to benchmark their practices and operations against others in their own industry. Understandably, direct competitors are often reluctant to share the secrets of their success with you. A more fruitful approach is to identify noncompeting organizations that excel in managing a particular work process (e.g., product/service warranty fulfillment, delivery systems, customer complaint handling) that you wish to improve.

Fortunately, several books are already available on how to conduct benchmarking studies.[2] Our mission here is simply to convince you of the *value* of benchmarking, which is essential to achieve customer-focused breakthroughs. By studying examples of customer-focused breakthrough inside other organizations, you gain a new perspective on your own organization's breakthrough potential. Benchmarking helps you see and feel new possibilities, which in turn helps you to set "stretch goals" that fall just within the range of achievability. Benchmarking also shows you pathways to breakthroughs that would otherwise never occur to you. Perhaps most significantly, benchmarking makes your stretch goals *credible*. It enables you to say to your people, "If others have done it, so can we."

Organizations that have embraced *hoshin* place extraordinary emphasis on planning. This reflects their leaders' fundamental belief that by investing the time and effort required to conduct systematic benchmarking and by involving large numbers of employees to create the breakthrough objectives, the organization has laid a foundation needed to support the next phase, deploying the breakthrough plan.

2 ■ DEPLOYING THE BREAKTHROUGH PLAN

Based on what you've gleaned from The Voice of the Customer, The Voice of the Employee, The Voice of the Process, marketplace trends, and your benchmarking studies, you have articulated your three to five breakthrough objectives. The next order of business is deploying the breakthrough plan. This is accomplished in four steps:

• *Identify* the critical few work processes most vital to achieve your breakthrough objectives.

- *Focus* quality improvement on these strategically vital aspects of your operations.
- *Document* your commitments.
- *Balance* functional vs. cross-functional process improvement activity.

Xerox, Business Process List

Market Management

- Market selection and analysis
- Segments and customer requirements understanding
- Customer requirements management
- Market planning
- Marketing support
- Marketing communications
- Market tracking

Customer Engagement

- Sales territory planning
- Prospecting management
- Enterprise management
- Agreement development
- Agreement management
- Customer support

Order Fulfillment

- Order processing
- Customer preparation
- Staging and pre-installation
- Delivery/removal
- Installation/deinstallation
- Product production

Billing & Collection

- Invoicing
- Banking operations
- Cash application
- Collection
- Third-party leasing
- Administration

Product Maintenance

- Service call management
- Service dispatching
- Product servicing
- Service call closure
- Product maintenance planning
- Product performance monitoring
- Technical information provision
- Service coverage planning

Financial Management

- Financial planning
- Financial analysis and reporting
- Financial outlook
- Tax planning and management
- Accounting operations
- Financial auditing
- Disbursements
- Financial asset/cash planning
- Financial asset control

Inventory Management and Logistics

- Inventory planning
- Logistics and physical distribution planning
- Logistics operations and material control
- Delivery management and order satisfaction
- Supplier management

Business Management

- Business strategy development
- Business planning
- Business process and operations management
- Process specifications
- Coordination and integration
- Inspection
- Benchmarking
- Process improvement

Information Technology Management

- Information strategy planning
- Business solution development
- Technical environment management
- Information integration management
- Technology management

Human Resource Management

- Manpower requirements planning
- Hiring and assignment
- Benefits and compensation management
- Personnel management
- Work force preparedness
- Employee communications

IDENTIFYING THE CRITICAL FEW

This business process list, drawn from *hoshin* materials used within Xerox, is a good representation of the various work processes one typically finds within major business organizations. To identify the few processes most critical to achieve your targeted breakthroughs, you must assess which ones offer the greatest potential to delight your customers.

For example, if you have learned that your customers would value a dramatic reduction in your delivery time, the "order fulfillment" and "inventory management and logistics" work processes would presumably be critical. If, on the other hand, the objective is to eliminate service calls during the first 90 days after product installation (perhaps through free on-site implementation consulting), you might wish to target the "market management" and "customer engagement" work processes.

CASCADING GOALS

Next, you must focus quality improvement efforts in each function and unit of your organization on the targeted work processes. This can be accomplished through an approach we call Cascading Goals.

Within Varian Associates, Inc. (a leading electronics manufacturer), this cascading goal helps focus quality improvement throughout an entire business unit, all the way down to the work group level.[3]

CORPORATE GOAL:

Reduce cycle time for delivery of new products to less than 140 days.

MATERIALS DEPARTMENT GOAL:

Reduce vendor lead time to less than 60 days.

PURCHASING WORK GROUP GOAL:

Establish value-managed (i.e., Partnering) relationships with 75 percent of producers of production parts.

The breakthrough objective, clearly stated in this instance, is to reduce new product delivery time to 140 days or less. The Materials Department has set its own corresponding goal, appropriately narrowed to the segment of the targeted work process on which it has the greatest impact. Finally, within the Materials Department, the Purchasing work group will focus its quality improvement efforts on redefining its relationships with vendors—a specific, measurable project.

Under *hoshin,* this cascade is repeated in other departments and within other work groups throughout the organization. Thus, company-wide quality action is focused on redefining or improving operations to achieve a handful of strategically significant breakthrough opportunities.

DOCUMENTATION AND MEASUREMENT

The focus captured in your cascading goals must then be documented, and appropriate measures should be identified to help you gauge your success in reaching the targeted objectives at each level of your organization. Over the next few pages, we present three simple forms that Xerox Corporation's U.S. Marketing Group uses to do just that.

The first form shows the U.S. Marketing Group's corresponding objectives and measures arrayed next to Xerox's corporate-wide priorities (far left) for 1991. The second form is used by each of the Family Groups within the U.S. Marketing Group for the same purpose, driving articulation of strategically vital objectives (and corresponding measures) one level down into the organization. As illustrated by the third and final form, Xerox's corporate-wide priorities

Xerox, Managing for Results
U.S. Marketing Group (USMG)

1991 Priorities	Objectives	Measurements
Customer Satisfaction	Become the number one vendor in the industry for customer satisfaction and achieve customer retention and billing quality objectives.	• % customers satisfied (CSMS) • % customers retained • % error-free invoices
Business Results	Achieve our profit and cash targets via strategies that focus on segmented customer requirements and drive profitable revenue and market share growth.	• % profit plan • % revenue plan • % lease and sale install plan • % cash plan
Employee Satisfaction	Increase employee satisfaction and motivation and continue to improve the work environment.	• % employees satisfied (ESMS) • % employees retained • % BWF plan
Management/ Business Process	Continue implementation of the quality intensification strategy and our business process improvement and simplification efforts. Drive towards improving our work processes and reducing errors.	• Quality intensification plans documented and implemented • Business process error reduction levels achieved • Process reengineering milestones achieved • Best practices process implemented; at least one best practice implemented in all organizations

eventually cascade all the way down to each individual manager.

Therefore, every manager sees *in writing* what is expected of Xerox Corporate, the U.S. Marketing Group, the Family Group,

Xerox, Managing for Results
U.S. Marketing Group (USMG)
Setting Family Group Objectives

1991 Priorities	Objectives	Measurements
Customer Satisfaction (applies to both external and internal customers)	• • •	• • •
Business Results (applies to achievement of revenue profit cash goals and/or reduction in expense and utilization of assets and resources)	• • •	• • •
Employee Satisfaction (applies to improvements in employee satisfaction; objectives required for all managers; self-development objectives required for all employees)	• • •	• • •
Management/Business Process (applies to the utilization of Leadership Through Quality tools and processes to reduce errors and improve business results)	• • •	• • •

and him or her personally in the coming year. What's more, every manager knows what measures will be used to determine whether those objectives were reached.[4]

Xerox, Managing for Results
U.S. Marketing Group (USMG)
Setting Individual Objectives

1991 Priorities	Objectives	Measurements
Customer Satisfaction	• • •	• • •
Business Results	• • •	• • •
Employee Satisfaction	• • •	• • •
Management/ Business Process	• • •	• • •

Balanced Attack

You need not be the Marquess of Queensberry to know that every competent boxer commands two basic punches—a straight jab and a powerful roundhouse hook. The jab is applied frequently to probe and wear down the opponent's defenses. The hook, in contrast, is thrown only when the boxer perceives a significant opening. To throw the hook too often is to waste energy while exposing oneself to a counter punch.

In the vernacular of boxing, then, we find that most business organizations pursue quality improvement breakthroughs with one hand tied behind their backs. *All* their punches are roundhouse hooks. True, they may score some early successes with this approach. But inevitably, they tire, grow discouraged, and threaten to throw in the towel.

The roundhouse hook of quality improvement is the cross-functional "tiger team" (sometimes called process management team or task force). Executives handpick high-powered individuals from various departments, form them into a tiger team, and instruct them to attack a specific problem or pursue a targeted opportunity.

The tiger team *is* a remarkably potent weapon for achieving quality breakthroughs. It is especially effective for bursting holes through the functional "chimneys" that divide most organizations, for destroying inefficient or obstructive work flows, and for tearing down other structural barriers to peak performance. In a dramatic symbol of this form of quality management, Lee Iacocca once "blew up" Chrysler's disbanded Research & Development Center, personally pushing down on the plunger that detonated the demolition charges.

However, the structures and work flows that tiger teams tear down must eventually be replaced with new ones. (There is no such thing as a business organization without structures and work flows.) And with the new structures will come new problems and new opportunities for improvement. Will you then convene *more* cross-functional tiger teams? How many times can you apply this approach before your people tire or rebel? (For that matter, how many more buildings can Mr. Iacocca blow up before the neighbors complain about the noise?)

Intriguingly, while large numbers of tiger teams now operate within many U.S. firms, one finds relatively few tiger teams in Japan. The best Japanese companies resort to this "unnatural" approach only under extraordinary circumstances.[5] Yet year after year, these very same companies delight their customers, gobble up market share, and reinforce their reputation for quality.

How do they do it? They effectively apply the "straight jab" of quality improvement. That is, they constantly pound their way toward strategically vital breakthroughs by making their *existing* structures and work flows perform better—much better—with each new year. Instead of leaving work process improvement to the occasional cross-functional task force, they make it part and parcel of everyone's job, so targeted improvements are pursued in each and every function, each and every day.

Some types of breakthroughs should always be pursued by people working within their natural functions. Breakthrough improvements in safety, for example, are often most attainable for employees who understand the safety hazards inherent in their respective departments. These individuals also have the most immediate motivation to achieve safety breakthroughs. Similar logic would apply to a *hoshin* calling for the elimination of erroneous data entry into a shared information management system. Since the data entered is often technical or specific to a given function, employees within each department may be the only ones able to pinpoint what erroneous data looks like in their area. And they are clearly in the best position to analyze and identify the origins of their bad data.

Breakthrough Leadership

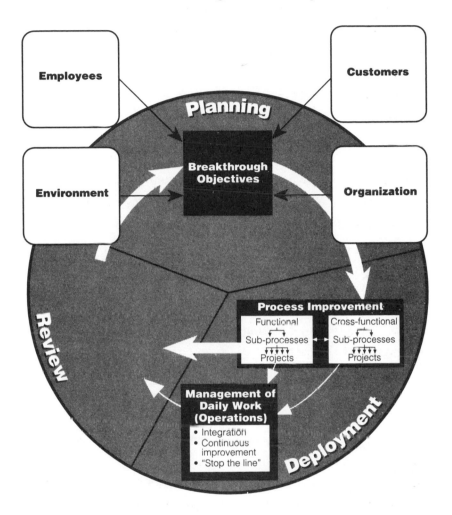

Also, note that your function-by-function pursuit of customer-focused breakthroughs *will* increase interdepartmental awareness and integration since, to fulfill their own objectives, most departments must interact with "internal" customers and suppliers from other functions. To completely eliminate erroneous data, each department needs to interact with other departments that supply it with information and with the internal customers who use the data that they themselves provide. Thus, cross-functional communication and work process improvement efforts take place among all functions, not just between departments represented on tiger teams.

Some work processes such as new product development or customer complaint handling are by nature so highly cross-functional that the tiger team approach will still be most effective. The same is true if major structural or procedural overhauls are required for your organization to perform at breakthrough levels.

In summary, your most critical work processes will likely cut across more than one department or function. But employees do not *always* have to take off their Sales, Finance, Operations, Customer Service, or Manufacturing hats to deliver high-impact quality improvements. As your TQM process matures, you will want to consciously balance your tiger team efforts with the more sustainable function-by-function pursuit of customer-focused breakthrough, and thus translate the momentum from your early tiger team successes into a more universal, sustained, and *ingrained* pursuit of customer-focused breakthrough. This is the essence of what Federal Express has done, and with impressive results.

Focus on the SQI

The focus for organization-wide quality improvement at Federal Express has been provided by the company's "Service Quality Indicator" or SQI, which tracks work process failures that lead to customer dissatisfaction.

"We had always tracked at least one important quality indicator: on-time delivery," says John West, manager of quality at Federal Express. "After all, 'on time, every time' is the basic premise of our service. We assumed that on-time delivery was what customers expected from us. No more, no less."

However, input from customers led Federal Express to revisit this assumption. "The truth is, our customers expect much more from us than on-time package delivery," Mr. West says. "They also want us to make timely pickups, provide an accurate bill, deliver their packages undamaged, and report the status of packages in transit. So, from our customers' perspective, a single quality standard like 'on-time delivery' just wasn't adequate."

In response, Federal Express developed the SQI, which tracks not one but twelve "events" (work process failures) that lead to customer dissatisfaction. Furthermore, each event is weighted to reflect the degree to which it negatively affects the customer. For example, a missed package pickup or lost package is weighted at ten points, each package delivered late on the wrong day produces five SQI points, and an invoice adjustment (i.e., the invoice was not correct the first time) generates one SQI point.

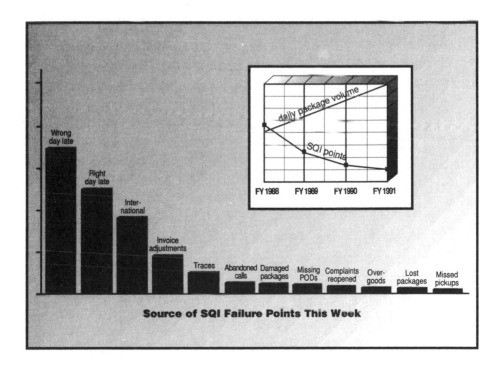

FY 1988　FY 1989　FY 1990　FY 1991

Source of SQI Failure Points This Week

The SQI score reflects the real number, *not* an average of service or work process failures that occur each day. So as package volume grows, it becomes that much harder to reduce the number of daily SQI points. (Imagine trying to shave fifteen points from your golf score while someone stretches the course from eighteen to twenty-two holes.)

The SQI drives an intense company-wide focus on the relatively few instances where service breaks down. SQI results are broadcast weekly over FXTV, the company's private television network, so everyone can track Federal Express's progress toward the ultimate goal: an SQI score of zero.

To identify and attack the process problems that actually cause the twelve service failures tracked in the SQI, Federal Express set up twelve cross-functional tiger teams, which they called "root-cause teams." Each was led by an officer or director of the company.

Brenda Brigman, senior quality administrator for Domestic Ground Operations when Federal Express commissioned this executive-led effort, points to the "Wrong Day Late" (WDL) and "Right Day Late" (RDL) root-cause teams to illustrate how the approach cascaded down through the organization to involve hundreds and sometimes thousands of employees in targeted quality improvement efforts.

"First, the WDL-RDL root-cause teams used flowcharting and other skills from our quality training to analyze the process by which packages move through our systems," Ms. Brigman explains. "They saw there were certain points in the flow where the process tended to either slow up or break down, which led to late package delivery."

Further analysis suggested that most of these process breakdowns and delays were brought about by a handful of recurring root causes—mis-sorts, labeling errors, missed aircraft, and scanning errors. Subteams were then formed to delve further into each of the possible root causes identified and, if possible, to recommend ways to eliminate those causes. These subteams were led by either vice presidents or managing directors.

Ms. Brigman says that once the root-cause teams and their subteams had completed their analyses and made their recommendations, the company's service assurance managers (or "SAMs") stepped to the fore.

"The service assurance manager's job is to help our people—throughout our Memphis hub and especially out in the districts and in our local field depots—to implement the root-cause teams' solutions in their daily work. It's a very tough job. But our SAMs are nominated by senior managers and selected by managing directors, so it's also a special privilege," she notes. Each SAM is placed on eighteen-month assignment, during which time he or she reports directly to the executive in charge of the organization. The assignment, therefore, provides an excellent development opportunity for the SAM. And the implementation effort is brought under the direct oversight of the senior line managers who run the company's major functions and divisions and are responsible for its various local operations.

"The SAMs work closely with teams that we call either service teams or continuous improvement teams. Within and across divisions, they reinforce the team problem-solving skills taught in our quality training and provide whatever other support the teams need as they go after the root causes of service problems," Ms. Brigman explains. "SAMs are on the front lines," she concludes, "helping people make the improvements they must make to lower our SQI scores in the categories targeted by our executives. And that's where we look for our results—in the weekly SQI report."

In autumn 1989, the Los Angeles metro district SQI registered 51.9 WDL-RDL points per 1,000 packages, a total that employees themselves deemed unacceptable. With guidance and quality train-ing support from local SAM Rosita Ross, a team of 27 L.A. metro employees benchmarked their local operations against the best per-forming stations within Federal Express. And several quality action teams were launched to eliminate the root causes of service failures within the district's ground operations. Monitoring its progress through weekly SQI reports, the district lowered its WDL-RDL SQI score from 51.5 to less than 19 in just over a year.

Thus, the drive to dramatically improve the targeted SQI work process measures initiated by senior management at the Memphis hub was deployed throughout Federal Express, even to far-flung locales. This company-wide combination of cross-functional and functional quality improvement efforts enabled Federal Express to reduce SQI service failures by 11 percent in the first year, even as package volume increased 20 percent. Each year since 1989, Fed-eral Express has progressed significantly toward its five-year break-through goal—a 90 percent reduction in the SQI.[6]

QUALITY IN DAILY WORK

In this discussion of Breakthrough Leadership, we have not yet addressed an obvious but vital point: Once you've achieved a breakthrough, you must *consolidate* the gain. Whether they stem from your functional or cross-functional improvement efforts, new and better ways of completing work must be integrated into your ongoing operations. Otherwise, even the most dramatic break-through will be of little value over the long term.

Thus, although management of daily work is not an explicit component of the *hoshin* concept, we emphasize it in our model for Breakthrough Leadership. You must make your employees keenly aware that any innovations they devise will be useless in the abstract. *All* improvement proposals should contain explicit and well-considered plans for integrating breakthrough ideas into the ongoing daily work of your organization. Whenever possible, breakthrough approaches should be articulated in the form of standard operating procedures. If a breakthrough cannot be captured in an SOP, it might not be as good an idea as it first appeared.

In the same vein, managers and employees throughout the organization should learn from one another and, whenever feasible, integrate into their daily routines breakthrough improvements generated elsewhere. Resisting work process improvements simply because they were "not invented here" is unacceptable. Unfortunately, many people find it especially difficult—psychologically and logistically—to embrace the breakthrough solutions produced by cross-functional tiger teams. Some local condition or restraint that the tiger team overlooked almost always crops up. And, because those responsible for implementing the tiger team's breakthrough are not vested in the idea, there is often little motivation to smooth out the imperfections. In contrast, when you pursue customer-focused breakthroughs in each and every function, the transition from breakthrough idea to application in daily work is virtually seamless.

Management of daily work also entails encouragement and support of your employees, ongoing *incremental* quality improvements, not just breakthroughs. Although less exciting than breakthrough, continuous improvement of all your work processes is every bit as vital to build and sustain competitive advantage as is empowering all your employees to "stop the line" (halt operations) if they detect a quality problem. After all, breakthrough performance in your targeted work processes will hardly enhance your standing with customers if quality slips in other areas.

3 ■ ENERGIZING BREAKTHROUGH: THE EXECUTIVE REVIEW

One of our all-time favorite *Fortune* magazine articles chronicled the wanderings of Sam Walton, the late chairman and founder of

Wal-Mart, as he traveled from one Wal-Mart store to the next, trusting only his eyes to assess how the battle was progressing on the front lines of his burgeoning retail empire.

What intrigued us most were the reactions Walton triggered in his "associates" (Wal-Mart's term for employees). They generally responded to "Mister Sam" for what he was: their champion.

> You can see in the eyes of some of the older ones that they think this may be the last time they will see their chairman and hero. So when he visits, they hug and squeeze him a lot, and when he walks out the door, more than a few pull out their hankies and dab at the corners of their eyes.[7]

THE POWER OF PRESENCE

Walton mastered an important force in business leadership, one that is too often overlooked: the power of presence. Like a general reviewing his troops, Walton energized his people *simply by showing up*. They knew that, instead of luxuriating in the confines of an executive suite, he had chosen to endure the rigors of travel (albeit piloting his own prop plane) just to be with them and to hear their views. And that said more about Walton's feelings for them, and about his faith in them, than mere words could ever convey. We believe that this aspect of Walton's management style is inextricably linked to the remarkable success of Wal-Mart.

Most managers seem to believe in the power of presence. They've experienced it themselves, either as leaders or as followers. Yet remarkably few managers attempt to project this power themselves. Why?

Many would tell you that they just don't have the time. Their management obligations keep them far too busy to "run around playing the leader." In response, we point to Jamie Houghton, chairman and CEO of Corning, who spends at least 15 percent of his time interacting with Corning employees, providing strategic direction and customer focus, and personally monitoring and evaluating the company's operations.[8] If a man who runs a billion-dollar corporation can find time to circulate among the troops, anyone can.

In truth, the most significant barrier to interpersonal leadership is probably not time, but *fear*. Most executives and managers have no way of knowing how employees will respond to them ("Will people really be inspired by my presence?"). In most organizations, no one has articulated any specific mission that would explain why managers are suddenly conducting site visits ("I don't want to come across as some kind of grandstander"). And no one has bothered to answer the most basic and obvious question of all: "Once I'm out there, what should I say?"

The *hoshin* approach to customer-focused breakthrough requires you to project the power of presence. You simply cannot hope to lead your organization toward fulfillment of your stretch goals from inside your office.

Fortunately, *hoshin* also provides a well-defined structure, rationale, and methodology to help you interact more effectively with your employees. The *hoshin*-style executive review minimizes dependence on intangibles like charisma. It is linked to a clear mission and supplies a powerful imperative for getting out of your office and into the field. And it ensures that you'll *never* have to wonder what to talk about with your people.

THE EXECUTIVE REVIEW

In the best Japanese firms, the executive review is a thoroughly orchestrated event. It is scheduled far in advance (in contrast to Sam Walton's habit of dropping in unannounced) and takes place at regular intervals, usually annually or semi-annually. Among its other important attributes, the *hoshin*-style executive review is

Breakthrough Leadership

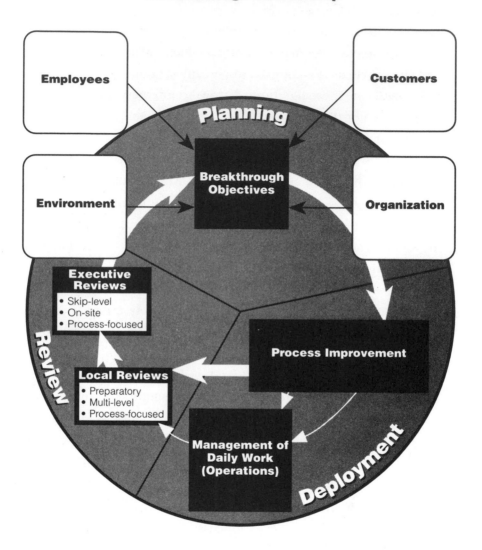

• a "skip-level" review, through which senior managers interact directly with employees rather than through the official chain of command.

• conducted on-site. The executive comes to his or her people to meet and work with them in *their* environment.

• focused on *process*. The visiting executive is at least as concerned about the "means" as the "ends."

As for the last point—the emphasis on process—the revered TQM teacher Kaoru Ishikawa suggested that executives and managers weight their reviews of quality teams as follows:

Results	10%
Selection of project	20%
Cooperation/teamwork	20%
Analysis of underlying causes and alternatives	30%
Standardization and prevention	10%
"Reflection" (what the team learned)	10%

Once on-site, the visiting executive shuns prepared presentations and instead engages as many managers and employees as possible in "give-and-take" discussions. Of middle managers the executive may ask:

"What steps are you taking to promote side-by-side communication and cooperation across functions?"

"Please summarize the employee feedback you've gathered since my last visit. How did you gather this feedback? What do you think it means? What actions are you taking in response to what you've learned?"

"I'd like to hear about your progress toward the process improvement objectives we agreed to last year. Which approaches are proving most successful? Is the training we've provided your people sufficient?"

"What kind of data do you gather from customers? How do you gather it? What percentage of your customer data comes from internal rather than external customers?"

Questions typically posed to employees include:

"Have our current process improvement priorities been clearly communicated to you? Could you summarize them for me?"

"Do you feel that you had a meaningful part in shaping our priorities? Do they seem appropriate to you, or do you think other objectives might be more important?"

"What quality improvement initiatives are underway in your work area right now? How are they going?"

"What new insights or ideas do you have to share with me?"

"Are you recognized for what you do? What forms of recognition have meant the most to you? What recognition would you value even more than what you've received so far?"

And always, of everyone, the executive inquires:

"What do you need? What can I do to help?"

Of course, senior managers will not always like what they hear during executive reviews. But only by going out and asking questions like the ones above can they gain a truly unfiltered perspective on the concerns of middle managers, employees, and (indirectly) customers. Executive reviews also provide the only realistic opportunity for senior managers to gauge the advance of work pro-

Executive Review, by The Numbers

The Canadian Division of Moore Corporation has adopted this fifteen-step procedure for its executives to follow whenever they conduct a Quality Site Review (QSR).

Quality Champions
MOORE · **CANADIAN DIVISION**

Step 1:
Become Familiar with QSR

Read the binder in its entirety. If you have questions, contact the chief quality officer in your division.

Step 2:
Determine the Review Dates

Contact the site at least 30 days in advance so that adjustments in work schedules can be arranged.

The site review should never be conducted as a surprise.

Establish a date by telephone, and follow this with written confirmation.

Step 3:
Develop the Schedule for Managers

Schedule about three hours with the site manager, and about 45 minutes with other key managers.

You do not need to meet with each member of management. Select a sample of 20-25%.

Step 4:
Develop the Schedule for Associates

Schedule time to meet with the associates in small groups of about 10-15 each. You should plan to talk with about 20-25% of the associates. These sessions should be about 45 minutes in length.

If you are visiting a site that has second and third shifts, be sure to allow sufficient time to meet with all three shifts.

Step 5: **Select the** **Sample**	Ask the human resources department for a list of managers and associates. Select about 20-25% from each list. This can be accomplished by selecting every fourth or fifth name.
Step 6: **Inform Associates** **about the Site** **Review**	Ask the on-site manager to announce the review to associates.
Step 7: **Meet with the** **On-site Manager**	Plan to spend about three hours. Record preliminary information.
Step 8: **Meet with Other** **Managers**	At the beginning of each session, talk about why you are there, e.g., not to find what's wrong, but to look for ways to continually improve the quality process.
Step 9: **Meet with Groups** **of Associates**	Explain your purpose, as above. Be sure that the associates understand how the information will be used. Establish an atmosphere of trust. Again, take notes.
Step 10: **Score the Review**	If you find that an occasional item does not apply to this site, mark it as N/A, and do not include it when computing averages.

Step 11: **Reach** **Consensus**	The team discusses each item, and reaches consensus. This is *not* accomplished by averaging the team members' individual scores. Instead, the team should discuss areas of difference and reach mutual agreement. Use only whole numbers. Record brief phrases to explain how the score was determined or to recommend changes.
Step 12: **Complete the** **Report**	The written report should be completed by the team before leaving the site. **This immediate feedback to management is critical.** *The team should not leave the site until the report is complete and has been presented to the on-site manager.*
Step 13: **Complete the** **Summary Sheet**	Transfer your scoring information to the summary sheet. Then compute the averages. Remember not to use the N/A items in computing averages. Make a copy of the summary sheet and the written report.
Step 14: **Conduct the** **Final** **Discussion**	Spend about an hour with the on-site manager. Explain the scores. Help the manager prioritize next steps. Remember, **positive** comments are important. You are the **coach!**
Step 15: **Report Your** **Results**	Each of the North American divisions has established its own reporting plan. Contact your chief quality professional if you are unsure of the details.

cess improvement, make mid-course adjustments, and even modify the breakthrough objectives, if necessary, to compensate for unexpected variables in implementation. Most importantly, face-to-face conversations with executives are often the most powerful stimulus for employees. Never underestimate the power of presence as a means of energizing customer-focused breakthrough.

LOCAL REVIEWS

As you might expect, local managers quickly learn to conduct their *own* reviews in anticipation of the executive visit. These local reviews reveal necessary data and insights, gauge local progress toward the breakthrough objectives, and prepare everyone to respond to the process management questions the executive is certain to pose during his or her visit. Local reviews should be conducted at multiple levels—by the top manager at the site (e.g., a plant manager), by department heads, even by supervisors of small work groups.

Executives in Japan and Korea often send members of their corporate staff out to sites to act as what we might call "advance men." Their job is to help local personnel prepare for the executive review, to build up their confidence, and to increase the probability that the discussions will be productive and beneficial for everyone involved. On our most recent study mission to the Far East, the CEO of Daewoo (the multibillion-dollar Korean conglomerate) told us, "If I cannot get all the information I need over the course of a two-day field visit, then my managers have not done their job. Local preparation is what makes *hoshin* work."

CONCLUSION

Study organizations in which quality does *not* work (as we have), and you will find a number of consistent shortcomings in how they Plan, Deploy, and Review TQM.

Their TQM planning, for example, typically yields twenty-five, thirty, or more improvement objectives, when it should align the entire organization behind a critical few breakthrough opportunities.

These objectives are then "handed down" to middle managers and employees with no effort to gain their input and commitment.

Worst of all, no one bothers to determine whether the targeted improvements will be valued by the organization's customers.

Similarly, in organizations where TQM fails, deployment activities rarely produce clear, timely measures and accountability. Individual functions, work groups, and employees have no way to gauge their own rate of contribution toward the specified improvement goals. And outside of the relative handful of employees selected to work on cross-functional tiger teams, managers and employees are not explicitly motivated to make such contributions.

The executive review element is often the least productive of all. We often find that executives are unwilling to commit sufficient time to on-site visits. The reviews they do conduct consider only outcomes (usually cost, production, or financial outcomes) with little or no regard for the fact that process performance determines these results. These "check the box" exercises do little to energize employees' improvement efforts or advance the organization toward strategically meaningful quality breakthroughs.

Underlying all these shortcomings, of course, is the absence of active, effective TQM leadership. For years, quality gurus have been saying to senior managers: "You are the key to making quality work." And for years, executives could fairly respond: "I *know* that. What I don't know is, what am I supposed to do?"

Now you have our answer. Become "the magic ingredient" in TQM. Do all the things you must do to win your people's hearts and minds over to the cause of quality. But don't stop there. *Use* TQM to shape your strategy and run your business. Stop setting financial goals and making budget decisions in the abstract. Adopt a whole new approach for setting business plans, deploying business plans, and reviewing the outcomes. Most of all, make the pursuit of customer-focused breakthrough your personal as well as organizational mission.

We promise you that you will not have to go it alone. You and your organization will need experience to grow fully competent in Breakthrough Leadership. But over time, consensus-based planning and deployment will become second nature. And the executive review will evolve from a tense ritual into a welcomed highlight on everyone's calendar.

More significant than the growth of competence, however, is the growth of faith. Your people's perception of what they can do will expand dramatically, not so much from what you say as from what they see. As their faith grows, they will stop waiting for you to challenge them with stretch goals. Instead, your employees will push you, demanding nothing less than everyday opportunities to test their limits. And with each customer-focused breakthrough they generate will come a radical redefinition of the terms "possible" and "impossible."

NOTES

1. For a description of the Baldrige Award, see Chapter Three's Notes and Appendix B.

2. We especially recommend Robert C. Camp, *Benchmarking: The Search for Industry-Best Practices That Lead to Superior Performance* (Milwaukee, WI: Quality Press, 1989).

3. The example is drawn from Varian Crossed Field and Receiver Protector Products, a Varian business unit. Please see *Center for Quality Management Journal* (Cambridge, MA: Autumn 1992).

4. To those who would equate this approach with Management by Objectives, we point to three significant distinctions between *hoshin*-style deployment and old-fashioned MBO. Objectives under MBO were generally mandated from above, while

objectives at the U.S. Marketing Group are set by those who are asked to achieve them. MBO focused almost exclusively on the results themselves, with little or no regard for *how* those results were to be achieved. *Hoshin* focuses on the means as well as the ends. Thus, the U.S. Marketing Group documents appropriately link Business Results to The Voice of the Customer (Customer Satisfaction), The Voice of the Employee (Employee Satisfaction), and The Voice of the Process (Management/Business Process). MBO habitually generated more objectives than could be realistically pursued at any one time. The U.S. Marketing Group, in contrast, has clearly chosen a "critical few."

5. This observation is based on more than ten years of research in various Japanese companies that have won the Deming Prize.

6. "Blueprints for Service Quality: The Federal Express Approach" (New York: AMA Membership Publications Division, 1991).

7. John Huey, "America's Most Successful Merchant," *Fortune*, September 23, 1991.

8. "Lessons in Leadership," *Harvard Business Review*, November- December 1991.

8 ■ CHANGING YOUR WORLD

Simple solutions are the best solutions. That is why we set out to write a relatively small book—one that would finally bring the "big picture" of TQM leadership into focus after just a few hours of reading time.

Our prescription for making quality work can be summarized in three steps:

1) *Identify immediate, compelling opportunities for breakthroughs in customer satisfaction.* Partner with key customers and use every other means at your disposal to tap into The Voice of the Customer, so you can achieve extraordinary insight into what would delight, not just satisfy, your customers.

2) *Lead your people in the pursuit of breakthrough.* Embody TQM values. Work *for* your people, and make both a personal and systemic commitment to hear and respond to The Voice of the Employee.

3) *Focus organization-wide process improvement on a critical few break-through objectives.* Use Cascading Goals, Catchball, Executive Review, and the other practical tools of *hoshin* to focus functional and cross-functional process improvement on strategically vital objectives and to continuously tap into The Voice of the Process.

If you follow our prescription, your organization will achieve customer-focused breakthroughs. You will dramatically enhance your ability to turn back any and all competitive challenges. And you will reap tangible business results sufficient to pay back your investment in TQM many times over.

However, we acknowledge that beneath the surface of our simple solution lay countless intricacies of implementation. In fact, if you do as we recommend, it will change your world. You (along with every other executive and manager in your organization) will take on a fundamentally new role and assume significantly expanded responsibilities.

Your primary job will be fostering customer focus. And to do that you will have to manage at least six interrelated factors.

The most significant factor is your customer-focus strategy. Ultimately, you will define whom you and your people will serve, what products or services you will provide, and what approaches you will use to ensure that customers choose you as their preferred supplier. To make this strategy concrete, you must then translate it into clear and consistent service standards that guide the behavior of everyone in your organization, function, or work group.

Chances are, your people will need some form of training and development to meet these service standards, which should continually "stretch" well beyond the standards you can meet today. You will also have to give your people more authority than ever to use their best judgment to achieve whatever it takes to delight the customer. And you must somehow ensure that you and your people

Six Factors for a Customer-Focus Environment

gather ongoing feedback from your customers and that your rewards and recognition systems encourage and support continuous improvement in the areas that your customers care about most.

GUIDELINES FOR FOSTERING CUSTOMER FOCUS
Here is a more specific breakdown of some of the action steps, which are keyed in to the six factors described above, that will be required of you.

STRATEGY

• Define your organization/function/work group's key customers.

• Give your employees direction on the products or services that should be provided and on approaches to use in developing and delivering these products or services.

• Target your methods for becoming the preferred supplier to each of your organization/function/work group's key customers.

• Develop your strategy by interacting directly with your customers and with others in the organization who know what customers need and how these needs can best be met.

ESTABLISH SERVICE STANDARDS

• Establish standards that clearly spell out guidelines for the people in your work force so they can delight customers.

• Set your service standards high enough so you can offer your customers unconditional guarantees.

• Make sure your organization is capable of delivering what your customers expect (if it is not, sound the alarm!).

• Communicate your service standards regularly and clearly in ways that inspire the people in your organization/function/work group.

TRAINING AND DEVELOPMENT

• Meet with the people you lead to identify the competencies they need to achieve customer delight.

• Spend time personally helping individuals develop their expertise to delight customers.

• Serve as a role model by treating the people who work for you the same way you would like them to treat customers.

• Ensure that the people you lead have the time and support they need for effective customer interactions.

AUTHORITY

• Authorize people to use their judgment, following the guidelines of your service standards, to take all actions required to satisfy customers.

• Provide the information your people need to make good judgments about how to satisfy customers.

• Continuously encourage individuals to take personal responsibility for delighting customers.

• Support individuals when they use their judgment and the service standards to try to satisfy the customer.

FEEDBACK

• Provide prompt feedback on how well the people who work for you are applying the service standards in their work.

• Help each person get feedback from customers.

• Provide up-to-date information from regularly conducted customer surveys and other formally collected customer-focus data.

• Help people use customer feedback to identify opportunities for improvement.

REWARDS AND RECOGNITION

• Select people for key jobs based on their individual levels of customer focus.

• Give organizational recognition to the people who best apply your service standards in their work.

• Reward individuals for delighting customers.

• Reward and recognize people in the organization for achieving customer-driven improvements in customer relationships or work processes.

SHOULD YOU "PAY FOR QUALITY"?

Of all these factors, none is more problematic nor more hotly debated in quality management circles than the issue of how to reward employees for improving quality.

KEY PERSONAL COMPETENCIES	EXCEPTIONAL		FULLY COMPETENT		DEVELOPMENT NEEDED		UNSATISFACTORY
CUSTOMER SATISFACTION • IDENTIFIES CUSTOMER REQUIREMENTS • MEETS COMMITMENTS ON SCHEDULE • RESPONSIVE TO CUSTOMER'S PROBLEMS • PROVIDES QUALITY PRODUCTS AND SERVICES	☐ ☐ Goes out of the way to make all customers feel they are respected and valued. Anticipates customer's requirements and is widely recognized as one who gives extra efforts to satisfy customers.		☐ ☐ Establishes with customers a clear understanding of their requirements. Meets commitments on schedule. Builds relationships of trust with customers by consistently exhibiting fair, dependable and ethical conduct.		☐ Is improving or needs to improve responsiveness to customers' problems.		☐ Normally fails to meet commitments on schedule. Lacks sensitivity to customer problems and usually does not meet customer requirements.
TECHNICAL EXPERTISE • USES KNOWLEDGE BASE EFFECTIVELY • ADVICE AND COUNSEL HIGHLY VALUED • APPLIES NEW INFORMATION QUICKLY • KEEPS TECHNICAL SKILLS CURRENT • SHARES IMPORTANT INFORMATION WITH TEAM MEMBERS	☐ ☐ Technical expertise is frequently sought by others, and is recognized as an expert in the field. Is perceptive and successfully applies knowledge to solve difficult problems, often by creative / innovative means.		☐ ☐ Effectively uses technical knowledge and analytical skills to solve problems. Is alert to changes in technology and job requirements and obtains the necessary training and education to maintain job proficiency.		☐ Is becoming or needs to become proficient in the technical and functional skills required by the job. Is learning or needs to learn to effectively apply technical knowledge to solve problems.		☐ Technical skills are not current. Demonstrates a lack of knowledge necessary for the job or may be unwilling to obtain new skills.
TAKING INITIATIVE • TAKES CALCULATED RISKS • DEMONSTRATES ENTHUSIASM AND PERSISTENCE • ANTICIPATES AND MEETS TEAM NEEDS • WORKS WITH LITTLE DIRECTION • MAKES THINGS HAPPEN AND IS RESULTS ORIENTED	☐ ☐ Moves out ahead of others in taking prudent risks, solving problems, and providing creative insights to all aspects of the work. Is persistent and enthusiastic about bringing ideas to supervision for acceptance and implementation.		☐ ☐ Anticipates the requirements and needs of others. Often performs tasks outside of routine responsibilities to accomplish job / objectives. Seeks opportunities to solve problems without being directly assigned the task.		☐ Is making or needs to make progress in working more creatively with less direction, in offering ideas and volunteering for tasks.		☐ Usually unable to work without specific directions. Shows little enthusiasm or persistence.
QUALITY COMMITMENT/CONTRIBUTION • IDENTIFIES AND ELIMINATES CAUSES OF ERROR • EMPHASIZES PROBLEM PREVENTION • SEEKS INPUT FROM CUSTOMERS AND TEAM MEMBERS • ENSURES SUPPLIERS CONFORM TO REQUIREMENTS	☐ ☐ Is a leader in commitment to quality and is seen as such by suppliers, customers and others in the group. Sees issues affecting quality long before they become problems and applies creative solutions of the highest standards.		☐ ☐ Identifies and seeks input from all customers and suppliers regarding their requirements and encourages input on ways to improve quality. Identifies long-term solutions rather than short-term fixes to problem.		☐ Is learning how to or needs to better relate quality to suppliers and customers.		☐ Shows little concern for providing a quality product or service.
TEAMWORK • STRIVES FOR TEAM RESULTS • GAINS COOPERATION FROM OTHERS • MAKES TEAM DECISIONS WORK • MANAGES CONFLICT EFFECTIVELY	☐ ☐ Is a valued and sought after team member. Aggressively supports team efforts, helps the team move through difficult issues, builds on the work of others, and seeks team results above personal results.		☐ ☐ Actively participates in team or group efforts. Builds constructively on the ideas of others to assist the team in solving problems. Discloses information freely and seeks information from others.		☐ Starting to understand the importance and value of team solutions to problems or needs to improve understanding.		☐ Has difficulty understanding the importance of teamwork or is unable to work on a team.
BUILDING EFFECTIVE RELATIONSHIPS/ COMMUNICATIONS • ENCOURAGES AIRING OF PROBLEMS • UNDERSTANDS CUSTOMER / SUPPLIER RELATIONSHIPS • KEEPS OTHERS INFORMED • RESPECTS FELLOW TEAM MEMBERS	☐ ☐ Is considered a highly valued member of the organization, in part because of the ability to work effectively with many levels within the organization. Appreciated by all customers of and suppliers to the group or team.		☐ ☐ Meets commitments made to others. Listens and responds to the concerns of others. Is effective in communicating and is respected as a credible source of information. Does not demean people; does not criticize people in front of others.		☐ Is learning or needs to learn the importance of building relationships and communication channels.		☐ Does not demonstrate a concern for others when working relationships are involved.

	EXCEPTIONAL		FULLY COMPETENT		DEVELOPMENT NEEDED		UNSATISFACTORY
SUMMARY OF KEY PERSONAL COMPETENCIES	☐ ☐		☐ ☐		☐		☐

The Pratt & Whitney division of United Technologies recently revamped its performance appraisal system to explicitly reinforce TQM. Shown above is a portion of the evaluation forms used for salaried employees. Managers are rated on key TQM leadership behaviors like empowerment and vision creation/deployment. And every employee's performance is appraised in terms of customer satisfaction, quality commitment/contribution, and teamwork. Copyrighted by United Technologies Corporation.

KEY LEADERSHIP COMPETENCIES
(Supervisors and Managers)

	EXCEPTIONAL	FULLY COMPETENT	DEVELOPMENT NEEDED	UNSATISFACTORY
	☐	☐ ☐	☐	☐
CREATING A SHARED VISION • COMMUNICATES GROUP'S MISSION • ESTABLISHES MUTUALLY AGREED OBJECTIVES • OPENLY SHARES INFORMATION • LISTENS TO OPINIONS OF OTHERS	Fosters and consistently achieves employee ownership of the group mission and establishes mutually developed individual job requirements / objectives that support the mission.	Works with next higher manager to connect manager's group mission with own group's mission. Establishes accountability with subordinates through job requirements that support the mission. Shares business information with subordinates.	Is beginning to relate or needs to better relate the next higher level mission and business objectives to own group.	Has not communicated the group's mission. Does not share information or listen to other's opinions.
	☐	☐ ☐	☐	☐
EMPOWERING OTHERS • DELEGATES RESPONSIBILITY AND AUTHORITY TO SUBORDINATES OR TEAM • ENCOURAGES PRUDENT RISK TAKING • RECOGNIZES INNOVATION AND IMAGINATION • ACTS AS "COACH," NOT "PLAYER"	Aggressively seeks opportunities to delegate responsibility and authority to subordinates, promoting and supporting their continued growth and increasing the value of their contribution to the group and the company.	Explains the scope of the job in broad terms, but not the method of accomplishing the tasks. When a problem arises, brings people together to solve it, rather than unilaterally developing a solution. Supports and defends subordinates' decisions once responsibility has been delegated.	Is learning to delegate or needs to delegate work and develop an environment for employee growth. Needs to encourage employees to develop solutions.	Does not delegate authority, encourage risk taking or recognize innovation.
	☐	☐ ☐	☐	☐
DEVELOPING PEOPLE • RECOGNIZES AND PROMOTES BEST PEOPLE • COACHES AND DEVELOPS PEOPLE • DESIGNS MEANINGFUL, CHALLENGING ASSIGNMENTS FOR INDIVIDUALS OR TEAMS • PARTICIPATES IN CAREER DEVELOPMENT	Views employee's performance and career development as integral to job. Subordinates are actively sought / selected by other groups for lateral and promotional opportunities.	Coaches performance toward achievement of results. Recognizes the importance of employee development and encourages activities that enhance skills and knowledge. Varies job assignments to improve breadth of expertise. Participates in career planning discussions with subordinates.	Is beginning to encourage employees' self-development. Needs to explore other developmental opportunities for employees.	Does not assist employees in self-development. Does not reward the best people.
	☐	☐ ☐	☐	☐
RECOGNIZING MERIT • GIVES FREQUENT, REALISTIC FEEDBACK • CONDUCTS CANDID PERFORMANCE REVIEWS • RECOGNIZES AND REWARDS RISK TAKING AND TEAM PROBLEM SOLVING • ADDRESSES POOR PERFORMANCE	Is a leader in drawing high performance from employees and recognizing them for it. Is aware of each employee's level of contribution and encourages continued growth through many forms of recognition.	Assesses accurately the accomplishments of subordinates, differentiates between performance levels and communicates candidly regarding employees' performance. Pay decisions reflect clear distinctions between levels of performance achieved. Effectively utilizes formal and informal recognition actions.	Is demonstrating increasing awareness or needs to be made aware of the importance of employee recognition and feedback. Needs to be more effective in contact with employees.	Provides little feedback. Fails to address performance issues.
	☐	☐ ☐	☐	☐
ACHIEVING RESULTS • STRIVES FOR HIGH PERFORMANCE STANDARDS AND DELIVERS RESULTS • DEMONSTRATES TECHNICAL COMPETENCE TO LEAD AND DEVELOP PEOPLE • PROMOTES TEAM INNOVATION AND CALCULATED RISK TAKING • SETS EXAMPLE FOR FAIRNESS AND HIGH PERSONAL STANDARDS	Is a recognized leader who promotes and demonstrates a high level of team participation and excels in implementing new approaches. Can be counted upon to deliver high-quality results with limited direction. Sets high standards and is sought after for unique assignments.	Completes most assignments on schedule and within prescribed completion times. Is a team player who effectively produces positive results on a broad range of tasks. Delegates and provides necessary follow-up to ensure a consistent accomplishment level.	Is beginning to develop and demonstrate overall group results that meet acceptable requirements or needs to improve overall group results.	Falls below acceptable standards and requires immediate improvement to remain in the present position.

	EXCEPTIONAL	FULLY COMPETENT	DEVELOPMENT NEEDED	UNSATISFACTORY
SUMMARY OF KEY LEADERSHIP COMPETENCIES	☐	☐ ☐	☐	☐

Note: Effectiveness in carrying out the corporation's policies in the areas of equal employment opportunity, affirmative action, and, where applicable, government contract compliance is to be considered in the appraisal for supervisors and managers.

Compensation strategy is always a complex and dangerous challenge, given the technicalities involved and the ever-present risk of litigation. But we need not be compensation experts to tell you that every TQM leader eventually confronts the question, "Should we pay our people for their involvement in TQM?"

Many (perhaps most) of those engaged in the compensation debate are opposed to "Pay for Quality." They offer a powerful and passionate rationale: "Improving quality is everyone's responsibility. It's a fundamental part of the job description, not something above and beyond the call of duty."

The strengths of this position are its simplicity and utter truth. In world-class organizations, working to improve quality is not an extracurricular activity. It is a minimum requirement.

Yet this truth does not necessarily rule out the option of monetary rewards for quality improvement. The experience of Grumman Corporation's Long-Life Vehicle Division, for example, shows that—in the proper TQM context—cash incentives can be a powerful tool for making quality work.

The Grumman Long-Life Vehicle (LLV) is the boxy white truck now driven by postal carriers throughout the United States. True to its name, the LLV is built to last. "Our design goal is a twenty-four-year service life," says Ed Hantz, Director of Process Grumman Quality (GQ), Grumman's corporate-wide TQM effort. "The major truck manufacturers probably think we're crazy," he adds. "Nobody expects a mass-produced vehicle to hold up that long. But we build a truck that exceeds customer expectations. And we deliver it at a competitive price."

Grumman manufactures the LLV in Montgomery, Pennsylvania, in a neat, compact plant nestled among cornfields, white clapboard houses, and softly-rounded hilltops. In Montgomery, the opening of deer season is a kind of holy day. Fishermen cast for walleye, pike, and bass in the upper Susquehanna. And 580

Grumman employees turn out 100 LLVs per shift.

The story of the Grumman Long Life Vehicle begins in 1987, when the LLV prototype excelled in the field tests run by the Postal Service (a trial so arduous, in fact, that no other bidder's truck passed the minimum requirements). "We had the best prototype by far. We deserved the contract and we got it," says Tim Gage, Human Resources Director and Quality Executive at the LLV plant.

Grumman's next challenge was to produce LLVs in large numbers. And fast. "We committed to a very demanding ramp-up schedule," Gage recalls, "but production of the LLV got off to a slow start. We were plagued with quality problems," he admits. "Too many vehicles that were scheduled for shipment were stuck in our rework zone."

Late in 1988, the Postal Service sent Grumman what Gage calls "The Letter." "Basically, it said that we were their worst supplier," he recalls. "That really hurt because, even though we were trying our best, we knew that what 'The Letter' said about us was true."

Stung by this criticism and determined to turn the situation around, managers and employees alike welcomed the advent of Process GQ. The TQM implementation began early in 1989 with plant-wide training in ODI's quality awareness and team problem-solving skills programs.

"Process GQ encourages everyone to take responsibility for the quality of their own work, and not to rely on someone else to inspect and correct your mistakes. It also gives each of us real power to change and improve how we build trucks. People here were hungry for more of that kind of responsibility," Gage reports.

GAIN-SHARING PLANS

On January 1, 1989, the LLV Division launched a Performance Award plan through which all full-time employees share equally in the financial benefits of quality improvement. More specifically, 50 percent of the cost savings gained through reductions in manufacturing time, scrap, rework, office supplies, and manufacturing supplies are paid out to employees in Performance Award bonuses.

"A gain-sharing plan can be effective if the amount of money involved is significant and if you provide a clear line of sight between the improvements generated and the bonuses earned," Gage says. "The formula for calculating awards shouldn't be too complex."

More than $5 million in Performance Awards has been distributed to LLV employees so far. In 1992, each worker earned a bonus of $3,400.

Individual employees can also earn additional bonuses through the plant's suggestion system. Grumman's LLV Division pays suggestors 15 percent of the cost savings generated from their suggestions, less the cost of implementation, with a $5,000 cap on each bonus.

This combination of TQM training, employee empowerment, and motivation through gain-sharing has produced extraordinary results at the Montgomery plant. Improvements documented since the launch of Process GQ include:

• Reduced time required to build an LLV from more than 42 hours in 1988 to less than 33 hours in 1992
• Reduced rework hours from 4 hours per unit to .1 hour per unit
• Reduced percentage of vehicles rejected (at final inspection) by more than two thirds
• Reduced frequency of truck breakdowns (in the field) by more than 25 percent

Most gratifying, however, was the turnaround in customer perceptions. Early in 1990, the U.S. Postal Service selected Grumman's LLV Division to receive its Supplier Quality Award. The correspondence informing LLV management of this honor praises the division's "ability and commitment to deliver a quality product," then states: "The USPS wants to continue to deliver the best mail service in the world at the lowest total cost. Grumman's performance has helped to make that possible." It was a far cry from "The Letter" that had so discouraged Gage and his colleagues in 1988.

This customer praise was soon followed with a solid business result: The Postal Service placed an order for an additional 43,000 vehicles, above and beyond the 99,000 it had contracted for originally. The new contract ensures that Grumman will be building LLVs for the Postal Service well into the 1990s.

Should your company implement a gain-sharing plan like that used by Grumman's LLV Division? We cannot say. In fact, most of the intricacies of TQM implementation defy blanket prescriptions. The "right" course of action is too dependent on local variables.

The LLV story does illustrate, however, the wisdom of confronting each question with a bias toward pragmatism rather than dogmatism. Yes, you must be passionate about quality. And yes, you must insist on active TQM involvement from everyone who works for you. At the same time, however, you must never let your passion for quality blind you to legitimate, effective options for making quality work.

CONCLUSION

As you consider the sum total of this text, you might very well be thinking, "Hey, this isn't rocket science." And you'd be right. In fact, none of the leadership behaviors we've identified as crucial to making quality work is beyond the reach of the typical executive or manager. World-class leadership requires no special skills or methodologies that you could not master.

We have shown you how to hear and balance The Voice of the Customer, The Voice of the Employee, and The Voice of the Process. We've described a clear structure and shared proven tools for focusing TQM on critical breakthrough objectives. We've explained how you must think about TQM if you are to wield quality as a competitive weapon.

Now that you grasp these fundamental truths and understand the action steps you must take, let nothing stop you.

You *can* make quality work. You *can* be a leader in your organization's charge to world-class performance.

Implementation Checklist

This checklist includes a series of right things to do. To score how well your organization is doing right things, total the number of points you have circled within each strategy. There are a possible 120 points for each strategy.

Planning

How effectively does your organization

		Not Done									World Class
a.	Gather and review data from its customers?	1 2 3 4 5 6 7 8 9 10
b.	Gather and review data from its employees?	1 2 3 4 5 6 7 8 9 10
c.	Gather and review data on its processes?	1 2 3 4 5 6 7 8 9 10
d.	Gather and review data from its political stakeholders?	1 2 3 4 5 6 7 8 9 10
e.	Align TQM data with business and organizational issues and priorities?	1 2 3 4 5 6 7 8 9 10
f.	Feed back data trends to key stakeholders?	1 2 3 4 5 6 7 8 9 10
g.	Develop a plan to achieve short-term TQM goals?	1 2 3 4 5 6 7 8 9 10
h.	Develop a plan to achieve long-term TQM objectives?	1 2 3 4 5 6 7 8 9 10
i.	Assign accountability for implementing the TQM plan?	1 2 3 4 5 6 7 8 9 10
j.	Develop ways to measure the success of the TQM implementation?	1 2 3 4 5 6 7 8 9 10
k.	Establish a TQM review process?	1 2 3 4 5 6 7 8 9 10
l.	Revisit the TQM plan to identify needed changes and document results?	1 2 3 4 5 6 7 8 9 10

Total points = ☐

Leadership and Commitment

How effectively does senior management

a.	Work together as a team to create the organizational mission, vision, values, and implementation strategies?	1 2 3 4 5 6 7 8 9 10
b.	Become educated in TQM?	1 2 3 4 5 6 7 8 9 10
c.	Train others in the organization in TQM?	1 2 3 4 5 6 7 8 9 10
d.	Become a visible spokesperson for TQM?	1 2 3 4 5 6 7 8 9 10
e.	Visit other locations throughout your organization to see firsthand how TQM is working?	1 2 3 4 5 6 7 8 9 10
f.	Reinforce TQM through rewards, recognition, and promotions?	1 2 3 4 5 6 7 8 9 10

		Not Done										World Class

g.	Maintain close and direct contact with key customers?	1 2 3 4 5 6 7 8 9 10
h.	Create an empowering environment?	1 2 3 4 5 6 7 8 9 10
i.	Make decisions and require others to make decisions based on data?	1 2 3 4 5 6 7 8 9 10
j.	Hold other managers accountable for implementing TQM?	1 2 3 4 5 6 7 8 9 10
k.	Listen to the voice of employees?	1 2 3 4 5 6 7 8 9 10
l.	Take ownership for key process improvements?	1 2 3 4 5 6 7 8 9 10

Total points = ☐

Infrastructure

How effectively does your organization

a.	Develop a TQM infrastructure?	1 2 3 4 5 6 7 8 9 10
b.	Create a means to manage the TQM rollout?	1 2 3 4 5 6 7 8 9 10
c.	Assign accountability for carrying out TQM?	1 2 3 4 5 6 7 8 9 10
d.	Identify, train, and empower internal TQM champions?	1 2 3 4 5 6 7 8 9 10
e.	Create functional, divisional, and regional TQM infrastructures (if appropriate)?	1 2 3 4 5 6 7 8 9 10
f.	Develop a process for reporting and monitoring TQM?	1 2 3 4 5 6 7 8 9 10
g.	Align the TQM infrastructure with the organizational infrastructure?	1 2 3 4 5 6 7 8 9 10
h.	Involve unions in TQM at the earliest possible time (if appropriate)?	1 2 3 4 5 6 7 8 9 10
i.	Enable teams to implement improvements?	1 2 3 4 5 6 7 8 9 10
j.	Use customer data when implementing or changing infrastructure?	1 2 3 4 5 6 7 8 9 10
k.	Identify, select, and train individuals to consult internally on quality implementation?	1 2 3 4 5 6 7 8 9 10
l.	Designate one person to be directly accountable to the most senior person for the execution of implementation details?	1 2 3 4 5 6 7 8 9 10

Total points = ☐

Focus and Rollout

How effectively does your organization

a.	Develop a TQM rollout plan?	1 2 3 4 5 6 7 8 9 10
b.	Target as a short-term goal the key processes you want to improve and measure?	1 2 3 4 5 6 7 8 9 10
c.	Target as a short-term goal the key managers who will implement TQM?	1 2 3 4 5 6 7 8 9 10

		Not Done										World Class
d.	Target as a short-term goal the key locations in which to implement TQM?	1	2	3	4	5	6	7	8	9	10
e.	Target as a short-term goal the customer priorities on which to focus?	1	2	3	4	5	6	7	8	9	10
f.	Provide "just-in-time" (JIT) training to support improvements?	1	2	3	4	5	6	7	8	9	10
g.	Target long-term rollout needs for headquarters, divisions, regions, and units?	1	2	3	4	5	6	7	8	9	10
h.	Target long-term rollout needs for more complex processes?	1	2	3	4	5	6	7	8	9	10
i.	Determine the appropriate time to involve customers and suppliers?	1	2	3	4	5	6	7	8	9	10
j.	Empower employees to take action?	1	2	3	4	5	6	7	8	9	10
k.	Select a few broken or critical processes and assign a senior manager to each one who is personally accountable for leading efforts to improve them?	1	2	3	4	5	6	7	8	9	10
l.	Set "stretch" objectives for improvement along relevant critical dimensions (cost, time, defects) for each targeted process?	1	2	3	4	5	6	7	8	9	10

Total points = ☐

Measurement

How effectively does your organization

a.	Review existing measures in light of TQM priorities?	1	2	3	4	5	6	7	8	9	10
b.	Develop a TQM measurement strategy and plan?	1	2	3	4	5	6	7	8	9	10
c.	Develop customer-driven listening strategies and measures?	1	2	3	4	5	6	7	8	9	10
d.	Establish new measures, as needed, to track customer satisfaction?	1	2	3	4	5	6	7	8	9	10
e.	Establish new measures, as needed, to track employee satisfaction?	1	2	3	4	5	6	7	8	9	10
f.	Establish new measures, as needed, to track process improvement?	1	2	3	4	5	6	7	8	9	10
g.	Establish new measures, as needed, to track organizational improvement?	1	2	3	4	5	6	7	8	9	10
h.	Develop TQM measurement tracking and reporting systems?	1	2	3	4	5	6	7	8	9	10
i.	Integrate TQM measurement systems with organizational and business measures?	1	2	3	4	5	6	7	8	9	10

		Not Done									World Class
j.	Use TQM measurement data for decision making?	1	2	3	4	5	6	7	8	9	10
k.	Use measures for proactive prevention rather than reactive corrections?	1	2	3	4	5	6	7	8	9	10
l.	Benchmark against world-class organizations?	1	2	3	4	5	6	7	8	9	10

Total points = ☐

Education

How effectively does your organization

a.	Audit employees' current skills and knowledge levels?	1	2	3	4	5	6	7	8	9	10
b.	Use the TQM training audit to assess current training options?	1	2	3	4	5	6	7	8	9	10
c.	Develop a TQM training strategy and plan?	1	2	3	4	5	6	7	8	9	10
d.	Assign responsibility for TQM education to a senior manager?	1	2	3	4	5	6	7	8	9	10
e.	Identify gaps between current training and TQM training needs?	1	2	3	4	5	6	7	8	9	10
f.	Establish a TQM curriculum?	1	2	3	4	5	6	7	8	9	10
g.	Identify training source(s) to develop and deliver TQM training?	1	2	3	4	5	6	7	8	9	10
h.	Make sure that training is rolled out first to senior management?	1	2	3	4	5	6	7	8	9	10
i.	Align training with daily work?	1	2	3	4	5	6	7	8	9	10
j.	Identify and train the best people to be facilitators?	1	2	3	4	5	6	7	8	9	10
k.	Develop measures of training effectiveness that reflect feedback from customers, employees, and processes?	1	2	3	4	5	6	7	8	9	10
l.	Benchmark its TQM training against world-class organizations?	1	2	3	4	5	6	7	8	9	10

Total points = ☐

Resources

How effectively does your organization

a.	Identify and fulfill TQM needs for financial support?	1	2	3	4	5	6	7	8	9	10
b.	Identify and fulfill TQM needs for staff resources?	1	2	3	4	5	6	7	8	9	10
c.	Identify and fulfill TQM needs for facilities and equipment?	1	2	3	4	5	6	7	8	9	10
d.	Identify and fulfill TQM needs for training resources?	1	2	3	4	5	6	7	8	9	10

		Not Done									World Class
e.	Identify and fulfill TQM needs for time?	1	2	3	4	5	6	7	8	9	10
f.	Clarify the relative priority of the resources allocated for quality as compared with other demands?	1	2	3	4	5	6	7	8	9	10
g.	Consider the needs of the customer when allocating resources?	1	2	3	4	5	6	7	8	9	10
h.	Provide ongoing education for employees to encourage them to develop skills and expertise for a variety of jobs?	1	2	3	4	5	6	7	8	9	10
i.	Incorporate quality into the annual planning and budgeting processes?	1	2	3	4	5	6	7	8	9	10
j.	Consider your commitments to suppliers when allocating resources?	1	2	3	4	5	6	7	8	9	10
k.	Consider management input when allocating resources?	1	2	3	4	5	6	7	8	9	10
l.	Benchmark against other organizations' allocation commitments?	1	2	3	4	5	6	7	8	9	10

Total points = ☐

Information and Communication

How effectively does your organization

a.	Gather and integrate information critical to TQM implementation?	1	2	3	4	5	6	7	8	9	10
b.	Audit communication needs?	1	2	3	4	5	6	7	8	9	10
c.	Assign a senior process owner to manage information and communication?	1	2	3	4	5	6	7	8	9	10
d.	Develop a TQM communication strategy and plan focusing on employees?	1	2	3	4	5	6	7	8	9	10
e.	Develop a TQM communication strategy and plan focusing on customers?	1	2	3	4	5	6	7	8	9	10
f.	Develop a TQM communication strategy and plan focusing on stakeholders?	1	2	3	4	5	6	7	8	9	10
g.	Communicate about both TQM processes and results to the entire organization?	1	2	3	4	5	6	7	8	9	10
h.	Integrate TQM communications with other communication sources?	1	2	3	4	5	6	7	8	9	10
i.	Measure the effectiveness of TQM communications?	1	2	3	4	5	6	7	8	9	10
j.	Benchmark TQM communications with world-class organizations?	1	2	3	4	5	6	7	8	9	10
k.	Communicate a personal statement from the president/ CEO about commitment to quality?	1	2	3	4	5	6	7	8	9	10

TQM

		Not Done									World Class
l.	Provide systematic and periodic updates to your customers and suppliers?	1	2	3	4	5	6	7	8	9	10

Total points = ☐

Systems Alignment

How effectively does your organization

a.	Align TQM with strategic planning?	1	2	3	4	5	6	7	8	9	10
b.	Align TQM with budgeting?	1	2	3	4	5	6	7	8	9	10
c.	Align TQM with rewards and recognition?	1	2	3	4	5	6	7	8	9	10
d.	Align TQM with appraisal and promotion?	1	2	3	4	5	6	7	8	9	10
e.	Align TQM with ethics?	1	2	3	4	5	6	7	8	9	10
f.	Align TQM with health and safety?	1	2	3	4	5	6	7	8	9	10
g.	Align TQM with marketing and communications?	1	2	3	4	5	6	7	8	9	10
h.	Align TQM with other key organizational processes?	1	2	3	4	5	6	7	8	9	10
i.	Align TQM with customer needs?	1	2	3	4	5	6	7	8	9	10
j.	Align TQM with employee needs for growth and development?	1	2	3	4	5	6	7	8	9	10
k.	Include quality involvement in everyone's job description?	1	2	3	4	5	6	7	8	9	10
l.	Tie your system for rewards and recognition to customer satisfaction?	1	2	3	4	5	6	7	8	9	10

Total points = ☐

Customer Alignment

How effectively does your organization

a.	Identify key customers?	1	2	3	4	5	6	7	8	9	10
b.	Develop a customer alignment strategy and plan?	1	2	3	4	5	6	7	8	9	10
c.	Establish valid customer requirements and expectations?	1	2	3	4	5	6	7	8	9	10
d.	Develop and use customer satisfaction measures?	1	2	3	4	5	6	7	8	9	10
e.	Create partner relationships with key customers?	1	2	3	4	5	6	7	8	9	10
f.	Link customer requirements to the development of new products and services?	1	2	3	4	5	6	7	8	9	10
g.	Develop and communicate policies and procedures to remedy service errors?	1	2	3	4	5	6	7	8	9	10
h.	Empower everyone in the organization to "delight the customer"?	1	2	3	4	5	6	7	8	9	10
i.	Gather continuous feedback from customers?	1	2	3	4	5	6	7	8	9	10
j.	Anticipate customers' future needs?	1	2	3	4	5	6	7	8	9	10

		Not Done									World Class

k. Offer TQM training to customers?   1 2 3 4 5 6 7 8 9 10

l. Benchmark to help achieve continuous improvement and measure the quality of the competition?   1 2 3 4 5 6 7 8 9 10

Total points = ☐

Supplier Alignment

How effectively does your organization

a. Identify key suppliers?   1 2 3 4 5 6 7 8 9 10

b. Develop a supplier alignment strategy and plan?   1 2 3 4 5 6 7 8 9 10

c. Establish valid supplier requirements and expectations?   1 2 3 4 5 6 7 8 9 10

d. Develop and use supplier satisfaction measures?   1 2 3 4 5 6 7 8 9 10

e. Use a vendor certification process?   1 2 3 4 5 6 7 8 9 10

f. Create partner relationships with key suppliers?   1 2 3 4 5 6 7 8 9 10

g. Anticipate suppliers' future requirements?   1 2 3 4 5 6 7 8 9 10

h. Give supplier awards?   1 2 3 4 5 6 7 8 9 10

i. Offer TQM training to suppliers?   1 2 3 4 5 6 7 8 9 10

j. Benchmark with key suppliers to learn how competitors are operating?   1 2 3 4 5 6 7 8 9 10

k. Gather continuous feedback from suppliers?   1 2 3 4 5 6 7 8 9 10

l. Empower everyone in the organization to improve relationships with suppliers?   1 2 3 4 5 6 7 8 9 10

Total points = ☐

Public Responsibility

How effectively does your organization

a. Promote quality awareness outside the organization?   1 2 3 4 5 6 7 8 9 10

b. Establish clear links between quality and ethics?   1 2 3 4 5 6 7 8 9 10

c. Establish clear links between quality and the environment?   1 2 3 4 5 6 7 8 9 10

d. Establish clear links between quality and health and safety?   1 2 3 4 5 6 7 8 9 10

e. Establish clear links between quality and image, marketing, and communication?   1 2 3 4 5 6 7 8 9 10

f. Support community service activities?   1 2 3 4 5 6 7 8 9 10

g. Encourage employee participation in community and professional activities?   1 2 3 4 5 6 7 8 9 10

h. Encourage customers and suppliers to participate in community activities?   1 2 3 4 5 6 7 8 9 10

TQM

		Not Done									World Class

i. Advocate your commitment to quality in the community through visits, speeches, and discussions with community groups?

1 2 3 4 5 6 7 8 9 10

j. Integrate responsibilities for public health, safety, the environment, and ethical business practices into quality implementation plans?

1 2 3 4 5 6 7 8 9 10

k. Assess public responsibility within different levels, locations, and departments in the organization?

1 2 3 4 5 6 7 8 9 10

l. Establish measures of the results of public responsibility efforts?

1 2 3 4 5 6 7 8 9 10

Total points = ☐

Summary Score

Record your total score for each strategy in the space below.

Planning _____

Leadership and Commitment _____

Infrastructure _____

Focus and Rollout _____

Measurement _____

Education _____

Resources _____

Information and Communication _____

Systems Alignment _____

Customer Alignment _____

Supplier Alignment _____

Public Responsibility _____

As you plan your organization's TQM implementation, consider how well you are doing right things right. The scores can be used to plan your implementation, evaluate priorities, or establish baselines.

Quality Progress

Learn From the Best

MAY 1990

Among Deming Prize winners, similar strategies appear again and again.

by
George H. Labovitz and Yu Sang Chang

REFLECT FOR A MOMENT ON THE WORLD'S most coveted awards. Better yet, compose a list. Include only the prizes that are universally revered, honors that have meaning throughout the world, and awards that identify a select few individuals or groups as the very best at what they do. What comes to mind?

Our own list was surprisingly short: the Nobel Prize and the Olympic gold medal. Most of the other possibilities we came up with were, for one reason or another, disputable.

Our point? Universally accepted standards of excellence are rare. The few that do exist are valuable because everyone can learn from them. By studying those who earn credible recognition for being the best in a given endeavor, pathways to achieving excellence can be identified. With just this rationale in mind, we undertook our study of companies that have won the Deming Prize.

Business success

For most companies, winning a prize is, at best, a secondary mission. The primary missions of the modern corporation are to compete, win new customers, and prevent the competition from winning away one's own customers. This is every bit as true in Japan as it is in the United States and Europe.

In fact, the Deming Prize and business success are closely correlated. Companies honored for achievement in total quality also tend to be leaders in their industry and conspicuously successful in competitive markets. Four such companies that have won the Deming Prize are:

• Toyota Motor Co., Ltd. This is the largest and most profitable auto and truck manufacturer in Japan. Favorable consumer perception of the quality and value of Toyota products has helped the company capture nearly 10% of world automotive market share. In the years ahead, Toyota appears likely to gain as much as 15% of world market share, a stake comparable to that held by General Motors.

• NEC IC/Microcomputer Systems, Ltd. A clear winner in the fiercely competitive semiconductor marketplace, NEC has also earned a reputation for having exceptional quality in a diverse spectrum of electronics and has enjoyed correspondingly dramatic gains in market share. NEC is pioneering the practical integration of computers and communication systems.

• Shimizu Construction Co., Ltd. One of the top five construction firms in Japan, Shimizu has recently made impressive inroads in the United States by developing golf courses, condominium communities, and similar projects. Industry observers note that Shimizu is exceptionally adept at managing properties after development is complete. Shimizu builds long-term relationships with its buyers. First, it offers financing and other services that ease the purchasing process. Then, it attends to customer needs that arise after the real estate transaction.

• The Kansai Electric Power Co., Inc. The most emulated Japanese utility company, Kansai helped open the floodgate of service sector quality initiatives in Japan with its total quality implementation. Kansai offers electric service at consistently low rates and has managed to shorten service interruptions significantly in comparison to other Japanese electric utilities.

Our research drew upon a variety of sources, including data and interviews compiled by Boston University's Asian Management Center, reviews of actual total quality program materials, quality management conference presentations, and informal exchanges with Japanese academicians.

The main source of information and insights for this article, however, was our ongoing series of personal interviews with Japanese companies that have won the Deming Prize. In most of the companies co-author Yu Sang Chang visited, interviews were conducted separately with total quality staff members and senior line managers.

The objective of this research was to identify total quality management practices that are consistently evident in the Deming Prize winners but rare in other companies. These distinguishing practices might prove valuable to competitive-minded U.S. corporations now casting an eye toward the Malcolm Baldrige National Quality Award.

A plan for success

To our surprise, one differentiating factor emerged almost immediately: implementation plans. Virtually all of the Deming Prize winners can point to clear, detailed, well-communicated total quality improvement plans, the likes of which are rarely encountered in U.S. or European companies.

Further, award-winning companies tend to communicate their quality plans schematically (i.e., in visuals posted throughout the company) rather than in burdensome volumes of text. Employees actually see the plan every day and learn of the company's goals through a medium they can readily understand and absorb (see Figure 1).

These total quality implementation plans are bound firmly by time, covering between three and five years, with specific annual themes or objectives. Examples of annual themes include reliability enhancement, strengthening vendor partnerships, and cycle time reduction.

Learn From the Best cont.

Significantly, most plans call for a general adjustment to changing conditions at least once each year. Feedback mechanisms on which these adjustments will be based are specifically mandated so the guiding principle of continuous improvement is woven into the fabric of the implementation plan itself.

Further focus is provided through the designation of a limited number of megaprojects to be completed each year. By stipulating specific megaprojects within the implementation plan, senior management effectively concentrates the organization's resources and energies on a critical few quality improvement objectives.

Finally, award-winning implementation plans tend to designate defensive and offensive quality improvement goals. Defensive goals are similar to those traditionally included in many U.S. quality implementation plans. They are directed at fulfilling the potential of the status quo (e.g., reducing nonconformance, eliminating cost overruns). Offensive quality improvement goals are, as the name implies, more aggressive in nature. They are directed at expanding the company's potential beyond the status quo, thereby improving its position against its competitors, increasing customer satisfaction, and building market share.

Often, the most powerful offensive goals are quite subtle. For example, most construction firms pay a great deal of attention to the durability and conformity (defensive quality goals) of the bricks used in their projects. But the builder who wishes to stand apart adds an offensive goal, using only bricks that weather in a way that is pleasing aesthetically. This subtle difference might not be apparent to customers when they buy the bricks, but, over the years, it will enhance customer satisfaction and set this one construction firm's product apart from all others.

In terms of content, award-winning plans tend to detail four main types of quality improvement activity: senior management activity, customer satisfaction activity, employee involvement activity, and training activity.

The executive's role

The Deming Prize-winning plans institutionalize senior management activity, defining an executive role that goes far beyond what one finds in most companies. Executives are required to seek out middle managers and solicit their input on quality improvement opportunities and goals. The theory, a sound one, is that middle management's commitment to total quality is vital. That commitment grows when executives take time to ask middle managers, "Where do you think we should go from here?"

In fact, an annual schedule of 30 or more field visits for each senior executive is not uncommon in award-winning companies. This is a significant personal commitment of time, travel, and effort, because these field visits involve much more than showing the corporate flag. For one thing, executives typically take time to gather relevant information before each field visit, using tools such as the *jissetsu*. The jissetsu is a report covering each site's quality targets, success in achieving those targets, causes for shortfalls in the total quality effort, degree of interdepartmental cooperation in total quality, and degree of user satisfaction. Plant managers must complete and submit the jissetsu prior to each executive visit, so the executive arrives at the field site with a significant body of data that can be expanded, challenged, and clarified in the ensuing discussions with middle management.[1]

To enhance these discussions, Japanese executives use interactive communication tools and encourage their middle managers to apply the same methods to advance the total quality process. One such communication tool is called catchball (Figure 2), in which the executive, manager, or any other member of a department or work group throws out the kernel of an idea for im-

Figure 1. Communicating Total Quality

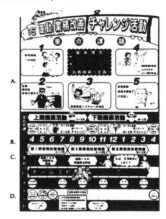

COMMUNICATING TOTAL QUALITY

This poster (from a Japanese insurance company) demonstrates that a complex total quality improvement plan can be communicated in a compact visual.

A. The guiding vision (black box at top center) emphasizes customer focus and is surrounded by five corresponding goals (roughly translated): 1. Retain customers through perfect execution 2. Achieve error-free processing of cash transactions 3. Make computer systems more customer oriented 4. Apply office automation to improve internal operations 5. Keep standard operating procedures up to date with customer needs.

B. A central feature of the plan is the time line, which tracks with the fiscal year from April to April.

C. The two graphic bars immediately below the time line designate activities for senior management (policy deployment) and sales personnel, respectively. The next graphic bar illustrates planned activities of cross-functional teams composed of main office and branch office personnel.

D. The bottom section of the poster indicates key events included in the plan, such as steering committee meetings, training schedules, corporate-wide recognition events, and quality team meetings.

proving quality. Someone might say, for example: "Imagine how happy our customers would be if we never again asked them to fill out a form."

Chances are, the idea will be impractical when first expressed. The information gathered on forms, to follow this example, might be required for the company to understand and meet customer needs. But, instead of discarding the idea, Japanese executives ask their people to "catch" it, reflect on it, improve it, and then pass it on to others, who will develop the idea further through the same process.

Catchball takes practice, just as a child must practice to become adept at throwing and catching a ball. But, as people become comfortable with the technique—and as everyone in the company learns that their ideas will indeed be caught, nurtured, and developed—catchball generates a steady stream of quality improvement innovations.

Within a week after the field visit, the executive writes a commentary for the chairperson and the corporation's total quality department, so each plant manager's performance is very much on the record. As you can well imagine, an executive visit does more to reinforce the importance of total quality than could 100 powerfully worded memorandums.

Keeping all customers satisfied

Customer satisfaction activity, the second main area addressed in most plans, is distinguished by a high degree of systematization and integration across functions. The plan identifies and assigns specific tasks and responsibilities to virtually all departments and sections because the participation of all parts of the company is needed to achieve customer satisfaction. Further, most award-winning plans stipulate regular gatherings of middle managers to ensure that customer satisfaction breakthroughs (as well as incremental advances) achieved in one area are replicated throughout the company.

Toyota and quite a few other Japanese companies use quality function deployment (QFD) to achieve the customer satisfaction goals articulated in their total quality plans. QFD, which is also used in some U.S. companies, has been described as "a set of planning and communication routines" that "focus and coordinate skills within an organization, first to design, then to manufacture and market goods that customers want to purchase and will continue to purchase."[2] Marketing, engineering, manufacturing, and other functions work closely together from the time a product is first conceived to pool their expertise and heed the voice of the customer as they develop new products and bring them to market.

Interestingly, the chain of customer satisfaction activity within award-winning companies often begins and ends with the sales function. The salesperson helps guide the general direction of the company by picking up valuable information about marketplace trends, hidden niches, and the like directly from customers and then passing these insights on to other company functions and the executive leadership.

Perhaps even more important, the salesperson helps each client, in effect, to develop his or her own requirements. So, in Deming Prize-winning companies, product specifications tend to be set in the field rather than in the factory.

Striving for total involvement

The award-winning Japanese companies are remarkably proficient at involving employees in total quality. Sixty-five percent or more of employees are active in total quality efforts within leading Japanese manufacturing firms, while U.S. Fortune 500 companies report that only about 25% of their employees now take part in corporate quality and customer satisfaction initiatives.[3]

The consistently high level of employee involvement in Deming Prize-winning companies is no accident, nor is it purely a reflection of the Japanese work culture. Every implementation plan we studied includes detailed provisions for employee involvement activity.

The emphasis on management's role is especially noteworthy. The plans specifically call on even the most junior of line managers to lead and champion quality improvement teams. The message is clear: managers must involve their employees in total quality to climb the corporate ladder. Middle managers, in turn, often serve as block advisers who oversee and nurture all quality improvement efforts in their areas.

The employee involvement activity components of award-winning quality plans also provide for individual contributions to quality improvement effort, most often in the form of suggestion systems. It appears that top Japanese companies have far greater success with suggestion systems than do their counterparts in the United States.

Consider, for example, the performance of Toyota's employee suggestion system for the years 1951 through 1986 (Figure 3). Toyota's suggestion system got off to a slow start. For the first five years, it generated no more than 0.2 suggestions per employee per year (a rate that nevertheless exceeds the average of 0.16 suggestions per employee now generated by suggestion systems in U.S. companies).[4] In fact, Toyota employees submitted relatively few suggestions until the early 1970s, when, in apparent response to the oil crisis of 1973 and other stimuli, the number of suggestions submitted and the average number of suggestions per employee skyrocketed. A similar leap occurred in

Figure 2. Catchball

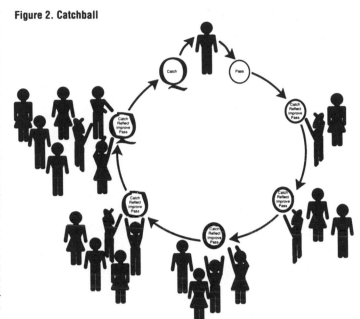

Figure 3. Employee Suggestion System

Year	Total of Suggestions Submitted	Suggestions per Employee per Year	% of Employees Participating	% of Suggestions Implemented
1951	789	0.1	8	23
1952	627	0.1	6	23
1953	639	0.1	5	31
1954	927	0.2	6	53
1955	1,087	0.2	10	43
1956	1,798	0.4	13	44
1957	1,356	0.2	12	35
1958	2,682	0.5	18	36
1959	2,727	0.4	19	33
1960	5,001	0.6	20	36
1961	6,660	0.6	26	31
1962	7,145	0.6	20	30
1963	6,815	0.5	21	34
1964	8,689	0.5	18	29
1965	15,968	0.7	30	39
1966	17,811	0.7	38	46
1967	20,006	0.7	46	50
1968	29,753	0.9	43	59
1969	40,313	1.1	49	68
1970	49,414	1.3	54	72
1971	88,607	2.2	67	74
1972	168,458	4.1	69	75
1973	284,717	6.8	75	77
1974	398,091	9.1	78	78
1975	381,438	8.7	81	83
1976	463,442	10.6	83	83
1977	454,552	10.6	86	86
1978	527,718	12.2	89	88
1979	575,861	13.3	91	92
1980	859,039	19.2	92	93
1981	1,412,565	31.2	93	93
1982	1,905,642	38.8	94	95
1983	1,655,868	31.5	94	95
1984	2,149,744	40.2	95	96
1985	2,453,105	45.6	95	96
1986	2,648,710	47.7	95	96

1979-81, the time of the second major oil crunch. Thereafter, participation continued to increase at a remarkable rate. In 1986, 95% of Toyota employees submitted suggestions. The total of more than 2.6 million suggestions submitted that year translates into an average of 47.7 suggestions from each Toyota employee.

How did Toyota foster such a remarkable rate of participation in its employee suggestion system? For one thing, all submitted suggestions receive a response within 24 hours from the employee's direct supervisor. Toyota workers never have to wait and wonder if anyone is listening to their suggestions. Further, good suggestions are systematically rewarded with gold, silver, and bronze medals or with membership in a Good Idea Club or another designation of honor. And, as in most top Japanese companies, a key senior executive is charged with making sure the Toyota suggestion system really works.

But the single most important reason behind the success of Toyota's suggestion system is illustrated in Figure 3 under the column titled "% of suggestions implemented." Toyota implemented a full 96% of the suggestions its employees submitted in 1986. This reflects both the high caliber of the employees' ideas and the sincerity of Toyota's commitment to act on the insights and suggestions of its people. Employees at Toyota know that the suggestions they submit will be valued and applied.

Consistent training

The final area addressed in the award-winning plans is training. In contrast to the disconnected bursts of quality-related training common in many other corporate settings, the Deming Prize-winners' investment in developing quality awareness and quality improvement skills is steady and ongoing.

Figure 4 presents a master quality training schedule from a Japanese manufacturing company that won the Deming Prize. The schedule mandates fundamental quality training for everyone in the company—from top executives through part-time employees—thereby ensuring that all managers and employees understand vital quality principles and can speak the same language. It also stipulates that new employees receive quality training within a few days of joining the company.

At the same time, the schedule clearly recognizes that quality training needs vary by level and function. QC staff members and specialists, for example, are required to complete far more quality training than any of the other groups. There is even differentiation within the QC staff group, with white-collar (clerical) training set apart from the courses for people in technical areas.

Just as important, senior managers in award-winning companies often take a keen interest in training content. This results in quality training that is, more often than not, exceptionally concrete. People are brought together to deal with real issues and to solve real problems that are of concern to senior management. The company simply uses these occasions to introduce new quality improvement skills and techniques.

Take these lessons to heart

We do not suggest that U.S. or European companies attempt to implant a Deming Prize-winning total quality scheme into their own operations. Clearly, a total quality process must reflect the realities of the company: its goals, its culture, and its people. On the other hand, it makes sense to draw all the relevant lessons one can from the best known and most honored total quality implementations, especially if a company hopes to gain such recognition for itself.

First and foremost, there must be a plan. Total quality improvement should be structured and scheduled in considerable detail. The plan should include offensive as well as defensive quality improvement goals. It should be communicated through visual media to every employee in the company.

The plan should put the burden of total quality squarely on management. Commitment must be obtained from senior executives to carry the total quality vision out of the boardroom and into the company's everyday operations. Middle managers should focus on unlocking the vast quality improvement potential inherent in the work force.

The quality plan should be used to unite diverse functions and elements of the company in pursuit of customer satisfaction.

Quality-related training activities should also be linked directly to both the offensive and defensive goals.

Even if a Baldrige Award or Deming Prize is not in their future, companies should take these few lessons to heart. They could be vital to continued survival and success in an increasingly competitive world.

References

1. Kaoru Shimoyamada, "The President's Audit: QC Audits at Komatsu," *Quality Progress*, January 1987.

2. John R. Hauser and Don Clausing, "The House of Quality," *Harvard Business Review*, May-June 1988.

3. ODI Executive Opinion Survey, as reported in the *Wall Street Journal* (Sept. 6, 1988), *Industry Week* (June 6, 1988), and *Quality Progress* (August 1988).

4. Yuzo Yasuda, *Toyota's Creative Suggestion Activity*, Japan Management Association, 1989 (in Japanese).

George H. Labovitz is president and chief executive officer of ODI, Burlington, MA, and a professor of management at Boston University's Graduate School of Management. Labovitz holds a PhD from Ohio State University.

Yu Sang Chang is ODI's senior quality counsel, a professor of operations at Boston University and director of Boston University's Asian Management Center. Chang holds a PhD from Washington University.

Figure 4. Master Quality Training Schedule

		Object		Course Name	Hours	Instructor
Compulsory training		Directors	All	Executive course (within company)	1.5 days 11H	External instructor
	Staff	Department and section managers	All	Department and section management course	4 days 38H	Specialized instructor
			Mgrs. with 5 years (+) experience	Refresher course	2 days 19H	
		Technical	All	QC (staff) course	4 days 32H	
		Clerical	All	QC (staff) course	3 days 24H	Instructor in each plant, division, and office
	Line	Supervisor	All	Supervisor course	3 days 24H	
		Group leader and circle leader	All	Group leader course	3 days 24H	
		Worker	All	QC worker course	one day 8H	
		New Employees	All	New employee course	one day 8H	
		Part-time Employees	All	Part-time employee course	one day 8H	
Specialist training		Staff	Selected staffs	1. Basic course (A)	4 months x 5 days/month 192H	Specialized instructor
				2. Basic course (B)	3 months x 4 days/month 114H	
				3. Reliability	4 days 39H	
				4. Design of experiment	4 days 36H	
				5. Multivariate analysis	4 days 36H	
				6. Others		

An Overview of the Deming Prize and Baldrige Award

Awarded annually by the Union of Japanese Scientists and Engineers (JUSE) since 1951, the Deming Prize recognizes outstanding achievement in quality strategy, management, and execution. Separate categories of the Deming Prize are awarded to individuals, corporate firms (companies, divisions, and small enterprises), and factories. There are other tributes to total quality excellence, but the Deming Prize is clearly the best known and most universally coveted of such awards.[1]

The prize is named after an American, W. Edwards Deming, who helped guide Japan's post-World War II industrial redevelopment. Yet American management has not been competitive for the honor. Only one U.S. firm, Florida Power & Light Company, has ever won the Deming Prize.[2]

The most obvious explanation for America's modest record in the pursuit of the Deming Prize is that U.S. and European companies have rarely bothered to apply for it. Until recently, the Deming Prize was not well known in the West, and the application process itself is rigorous.

In fact, non-Japanese companies were ineligible to seek the honor until 1987. But most informed observers agree: very few U.S. corporations could have qualified for the Deming Prize, even had they been eligible. American management has just begun to demonstrate the requisite commitment to total quality principles and practice.

Today, a handful of U.S. corporations might be ready to follow in Florida Power & Light Company's footsteps and apply for the Deming Prize. But a greater number of companies appear to be setting their sights on a goal much closer to home: the Malcolm Baldrige National Quality Award.

The criteria used to select winners of the Baldrige Award are in some ways different from those used in selecting winners of the Deming Prize. However, the two awards are essentially similar in that "both look for quality commitment throughout the organization, from the top down, including anyone with a relationship with the company, such as suppliers, distributors, and customers."[3] This similarity suggests that U.S. corporations now aspiring to the Baldrige Award can profit from an analysis of the quality management practices of Deming Prize winners.

References

1. An even higher honor, The Nippon Quality Medal, can be earned by companies that have previously won the Deming Prize and thereafter demonstrate five or more years of ongoing improvement.

2. Three U.S. corporations were previously associated with the Deming Prize, but each was recognized for operations run either by a Japanese subsidiary or through a joint venture with Japanese partners. They are Texas Instruments Japan, Ltd., Bipolar Department; Fuji-Xerox Co., Ltd.; and Yokogawa-Hewlett Packard Co., Ltd.

3. David Bush and Kevin Dooley, "The Deming Prize and Baldrige Award: How They Compare," *Quality Progress*, January 1989.

Deming Prize Winners 1978–1985

1978	Tokai Rika Co., Ltd. Chuetsu Metal Works Co., Ltd. (S)
1979	Nippon Electric Kyushu, Ltd. Sekisui Chemical Co., Ltd. Takenaka Komuten Co., Ltd. Tohoku Richo Co., Ltd. Hamakako Denso Co., Ltd. (S)
1980	Fuji Xerox Co., Ltd. Kayaba Industry Co., Ltd. Komatsu Forklift Co., Ltd. The Takaoka Industrial Co., Ltd. Kyowa Industries Co., Ltd. (S)
1981	Aiphone Co., Ltd.(S) Kyosan Denki Co., Ltd. (S) Tokyo Juki Industrial Co., Ltd.; Industrial Sewing Machine Division (D)
1982	Kajima Corporation Nippon Electric Yamagata, Ltd. Rhythm Watch Co., Ltd. Yokogawa Hewlett-Packard Co., Ltd. Aisin Chemical Co., Ltd. (S) Shinwa Industries, Ltd. (S)
1983	Shimizu Construction Co., Ltd. The Japan Steel Works, Ltd. Aisin Keikinzoku Co., Ltd. (S)
1984	Komatsu Zenoah Co., Ltd. The Kansai Electric Power Co., Inc. Yaskawa Electric Manufacturing Co., Ltd. Anjo Denki Co., Ltd. (S) Hokuriku Kogyo Co., Ltd. (S)
1985	Toyoda Machine Works, Ltd. Toyoda Gosei Co., Ltd. Nippon Carbon Co., Ltd. Nippon Zeon Co., Ltd. Uchino Komuten Co., Ltd. (S) Comany Co., Ltd. (S) Hoyo Seiki Co., Ltd. (S) Texas Instruments Japan, Ltd.; Bipolar Department (D)
(S) Deming Application Prize for Small Enterprise *(D) Deming Application Prize for Division*	

Deming Prize Winners 1986–1991

1986	Toyoda Automatic Loom Works, Ltd. Hazama-gumi, Ltd. Sanyo Electric Works, Ltd. (S) Nitto Construction Co., Ltd. (S)
1987	Aisin Chemical Co., Ltd. Daihen Corp. NEC IC Microcomputer Systems, Ltd.
1988	Aisin Light Metal Co., Ltd. Asmo Company, Ltd. Fuji Tekko Co., Ltd. Joban Hawaian Center Suntory Company, Ltd.; Masashino Brewery Plant (D)
1989	Aisin Sinwa Co., Ltd. Itoki Kosakusyo Co., Ltd. Toto Co., Ltd. Ahresty Corp. NEC Tohoku, Ltd. Maeda Corp. Florida Power & Light Co. Toyooki Kogyo Co., Ltd. Kobe Steel, Ltd.; Chofu-Kita Plant Maeta Concrete Industry, Ltd.; Honsha Plant
1990	Aishin Hoyo Co., Ltd. Amada Washino Co., Ltd. NEC Shizuoka Co., Ltd. Suntory Ltd.; Yamanashi Winery Aishin Seiki Co., Ltd.
1991	NEC Kansai, Ltd. Nachi-Fujikoshi, Corp. Hokushin Industries, Inc. Philips Taiwan, Ltd. Sin'ei Industries Co., Ltd. Niigata Toppan Printing Co., Ltd. Aisin Aw Co., Ltd.
	(S) Deming Application Prize for Small Enterprise *(D) Deming Application Prize for Division*

The Baldrige Award Examination Categories

1.0	Leadership	(95 points)
2.0	Information and Analysis	(75 points)
3.0	Strategic Quality Planning	(60 points)
4.0	Human Resource Development and Management	(150 points)
5.0	Management of Process Quality	(140 points)
6.0	Quality and Operational Results	(180 points)
7.0	Customer Focus and Satisfaction	(300 points)
	Total	**(1,000 points)**

Baldrige Award Winners 1988–1992

	Award Category		
	Manufacturing	**Service**	**Small Business**
1988	• Motorola, Inc. • Westinghouse Commercial; Nuclear Fuel Division	—No award given—	• Globe Metallurgical, Inc.
1989	• Milliken & Company • Xerox Business Products and Systems	—No award given—	—No award given—
1990	• Cadillac Motor Car Company • IBM Rochester	• Federal Express Corporation	• Wallace Co., Inc.
1991	• Solectron Corporation • Zytec Corporation	—No award given—	• Marlow Industries
1992	• AT&T Network Systems Group; Transmission Systems Business Unit • Texas Instruments, Inc.; Defense Systems and Electronics Group	• AT&T Universal Card Services • The Ritz-Carlton Hotel Company	• Granite Rock Company

Your quality advantage is built on five pillars of quality, which in turn are supported by a solid foundation of organizational values consistent with TQM. World-class organizations consistently excel in all of these critical areas.

Definitions: The Five Pillars of Quality

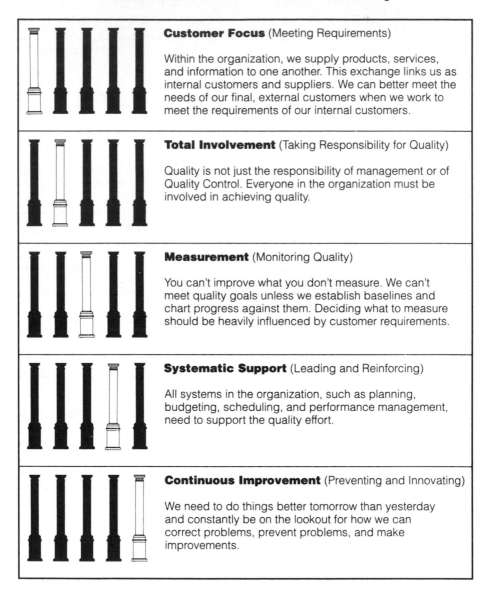

Customer Focus (Meeting Requirements)

Within the organization, we supply products, services, and information to one another. This exchange links us as internal customers and suppliers. We can better meet the needs of our final, external customers when we work to meet the requirements of our internal customers.

Total Involvement (Taking Responsibility for Quality)

Quality is not just the responsibility of management or of Quality Control. Everyone in the organization must be involved in achieving quality.

Measurement (Monitoring Quality)

You can't improve what you don't measure. We can't meet quality goals unless we establish baselines and chart progress against them. Deciding what to measure should be heavily influenced by customer requirements.

Systematic Support (Leading and Reinforcing)

All systems in the organization, such as planning, budgeting, scheduling, and performance management, need to support the quality effort.

Continuous Improvement (Preventing and Innovating)

We need to do things better tomorrow than yesterday and constantly be on the lookout for how we can correct problems, prevent problems, and make improvements.

SERVICE: Federal Express

Sorting out a mess

THE NATION'S NEWSPAPER
USA TODAY
NO. 1 IN THE USA

Hourly workers apply training in problem solving

By Martha T. Moore
USA TODAY

MEMPHIS — The fail-safe at Federal Express was failing.

To deliver absolutely, positively overnight, the quality-obsessed company has an elaborate system of routing, sorting, and tracking packages at its superhub here. About 750,000 packages a night are taken in, sorted and spit out to waiting planes within three hours. The backup mechanism is the minisort — a second process to handle packages that arrive late, are misdirected by earlier sorting, or are incorrectly addressed. It's the last chance for packages to make flights out of Memphis.

Not long ago, the minisort was a major mess: inefficient, costly and unreliable. Morale was low.

A team of FedEx employees, most of them part-time, hourly workers, overhauled the process. Team members put into action quality training received at FedEx. Their improvements have saved the company $938,000 over 18 months and won them the RIT/USA TODAY Quality Cup in the service category.

The minisort had always been a headache. The process was taking more than an hour at the end of every night, and as many as 4,300 packages a month were still missing flights. Missed packages are put on commercial flights. That expediting is expensive — $16.60 per package — and, for a company that guarantees overnight delivery, humiliating. The company was spending $875,000 a year on missed packages. Managers were so frustrated with the minisort that the company even abandoned it for a while — but rein-

stituted it when the cost of expediting packages soared.

Employees weren't any happier. A minisort assignment was viewed as punishment. "If you got on someone's nerves, they sent you to minisort," says Thomas Sit Jr. There was a lot of shouting, a lot of confusion and mountains of packages going nowhere. "It was just miserable down there," says team member Jeff Acree.

The 12-member team relied on a four step problem-solving method taught by Federal Express: focus on the problem, analyze the operation, develop a plan, execute the plan.

For five months, team members met weekly at work — and almost daily over breakfast after their night shift.

Minisort was a jumbled mess, in part because FedEx had grown so fast in the 1980s. Employees used to sort by memory. They knew the codes for each city. But as the company grew, cities were divided into several zones and employees could no longer remember all the codes.

The team first cut the number of workers assigned to the minisort. The staff had swelled to 150 workers, most of whom weren't sure what they were supposed to be doing. "They kept thinking, 'We need more people,'" says senior manager Melvin Washington, leader of the quality team. "We didn't need more people. We needed more organization."

The team cut the staff to 80 workers and armed them with an operating plan. An organization chart listed each night's workers, their jobs, their man-

agers, even where they were supposed to stand. By clarifying who did what and how, employees could accomplish more work with fewer people — and they enjoyed it more. (Federal Express hourly employees are guaranteed 17.5 hours of work a week. Lowering employment in minisort meant cutting extra hours, not firing workers.)

What the team did:

A team of FedEx employees — most part-time — reorganized the minisort operation for misdirected packages, saving $938,000 over 18 months.

What a judge said:

"

They assembled a team that used a methodology that appears to be reproducible throughout the company or throughout anybody's company.

"

— **Kenneth Leach,**
Leach Quality

The team persuaded workers in other departments to cut the number of packages sent to the minisort — from more than 10,000 to 4,000 per night — by stepping up their own quality control measures. "One of the hardest things was to get people to stop thinking, 'If we miss a package, minisort will fix it,'" Acree says.

The team made physical changes to make the job easier. Team members hung signs by each worker's station listing which package codes went on which flight. They added the flight number and destination to the sign so packages that reach the end of the belt without being sorted can be returned to the front of the sorting line faster. The sign change cut that time from six minutes to three. A traffic cop was appointed to direct the tractors taking packages to planes.

"It seems so simple," Washington says. "But it wasn't." Team members gathered information, listened to their colleagues' complaints and preached the new plan to skeptical workers in other departments.

"The hardest part was selling it to everyone," Washington says. But everyone was convinced by the results:

▶ The time spent on the minisort fell from more than an hour to an average of 38 minutes.

▶ The number of packages expedited fell from 4,302 in August 1990 to 1,807 in September 1990, saving the company $41,417 for just that month. In December, despite the Christmas rush, only 423 packages missed their flights.

▶ The reduced staff — and time saved by other staff — cut the payroll $28,544 a month.

Because Federal Express has a profit-sharing program, employees are sensitive to wasted money — and to the company's stock price, which is broadcast on TV sets that line the superhub's entrance hall. "You look at (the minisort) and think of the money that was being spent down here — and it was wasted," says team member Brent Barr. "You can't worry, 'Am I being paid for this?' You've got to think, 'Am I going to be here next week if I'm not thinking about quality?' "

Says Washington: "We did most of our work on Saturday mornings at breakfast, off the clock — that's how excited they were about getting this done. I'm sure there were many mornings when the (restaurant) manager wanted to run us out of there. We would sit there until 2 o'clock in the afternoon."

The team's improvements actually cost employees money — each member lost about an hour's wages a night, or about $50 a week, when the minisort finished earlier. But "at 4 o'clock in the morning, you just want to go home," Acree says.

Team members found the recognition from their company rewarding. "For management to listen to me, that's important," says Dawn Mason.

So was learning that the four step quality process they'd been drilled in really worked.

"When people started smiling down there," Acree says, "that's when quality started to mean something to me."

THE "FADE" PROCESS

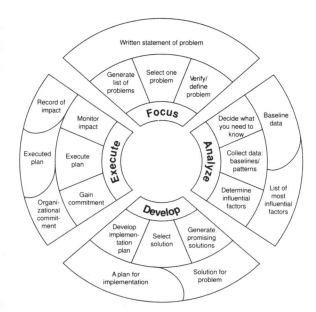

The "FADE" problem-solving process, used by quality teams throughout Federal Express, is also widely applied in manufacturing, healthcare, and government organizations. FADE is a central component of ODI's Quality Action Teams program.

THE WALL STREET JOURNAL.

© 1987 Dow Jones & Company, Inc. All Rights Reserved.

MONDAY, JULY 6, 1987

Keeping Your Internal Customers Satisfied

Manager's Journal

by George H. Labovitz, Ph.D.

In the ideal organization, every employee would have direct contact with paying customers and be effective in meeting their needs. But the reality in large companies is that most employees are shielded from customers, either by organizational layers or lack of proximity. The shop foreman in a Detroit auto factory, for example, may never speak with the Texas housewife who buys and depends on his product.

However, the foreman and other employees who lack direct contact still have opportunities to contribute to customer satisfaction. Every employee is part of a chain of internal "customers" and "suppliers" that ultimately extends to the external customer. The manager's job is to process work through the internal customer-supplier chain, helping employees play their parts in ensuring that the end product or service fully satisfies the end user.

At IBM, the notion of internal customers dates back to the "Basic Beliefs" articulated by founder Thomas Watson. "It has always been implied in our culture," says William Eggleston, vice president of quality. "And since the late 1970s, it has been explicitly stated in our management guidelines. The objective is to meet the needs of your customer, and your 'customer' is whomever your work moves to next," he says.

Jean Bernard, Bell Canada's vice president of personnel, says her company is actively building an "internal customer orientation" into its management style. "The terminology is becoming commonplace here," she says.

More than 10,000 Shell Oil employees have participated in a quality-improvement training program, part of which focuses on working together in customer-supplier relationships. "Shell's emphasis on the internal customer is paying off," says Vic Figurelli, manager of quality improvement. "It has already provided a common language that engineers, craftsmen, clerical staff and business managers can all share to get work done."

The formula for successful internal customer-supplier relationships varies. But it always begins with people asking their internal customers three basic questions: 1) "What do you need from me?" 2) "What do you do with my output?" 3) "Are there any gaps between what you need and what you get?"

Mr. Eggleston observes: "Throughout IBM, you find people setting 'contracts' at the internal-customer interface. Each contract contains explicit statements of what the internal customer expects and clear criteria for measuring success in meeting those expectations. We manage directly to the goals established in these contracts."

At Bell Canada, the assignment group processes service orders and assigns telephone-equipment installers to specific customers. "Assignment group staff rarely have direct contact with our paying customers, but our 10% error rate in assigning and scheduling installers had a direct and negative impact on customer satisfaction," notes Ms. Bernard.

Assignment-group managers met with their counterparts responsible for installations and service orders to address the 10% error rate. "First they tackled critical issues that could be solved or alleviated in the short term," Ms. Bernard says. "Then they looked ahead to explore all the aspects of their interdependent roles in satisfying our customers."

One activity required managers from different functions to work together to create "service maps" illustrating barriers to customer satisfaction, thereby suggesting specific changes likely to improve customer service. "The assignment group has since documented a tenfold decrease in their error rate, from 10% down to 1%," Ms. Bernard reports.

Mr. Eggleston stresses that the successful internal customer-supplier relationship is a two-way street: "Accounting is a good example. Virtually all departments supply accounting with data and in turn depend on accounting to process that data into useful information."

At one point, 3%-5% of all of the accounting department entries were miscoded at IBM. "That may not sound too bad. But because we make millions of entries each year, this miscode rate translated into more than 30,000 separate errors," Mr. Eggleston says. "Good management sense demanded that we take steps to reduce this figure."

IBM attacked the problem in terms of customers and suppliers, even though no paying customers were directly involved. "Accounting managers worked out a series of agreements with internal suppliers of the data their people enter. They did the same with the internal customers who depend on accurate information from the accounting department. Often, the supplier and customer were the same person," Mr. Eggleston notes.

Specifically, managers from the accounting department had three objectives in regard to their internal customers. First, they negotiated acceptable levels of accuracy for information coming into and going out of accounting. Second, they identified and developed the tools required to meet their accuracy commitments. For example, accounting provided a personal-computer software program that helped internal customers screen their own data for errors before submitting them to accounting. Third, they established feedback mechanisms by which accounting and its internal customers could identify and return erroneous information to each other and offer suggestions on how to prevent the errors from reoccurring.

"Managers in other parts of the company were a little surprised to have their data supply errors pointed out by accounting," Mr. Eggleston recalls. "But they quickly saw that this was the first step in a whole new process designed to help accounting provide more accurate information." The result? "We have reduced the miscoding rate to less than 1%."

Management is a key to reaping the benefits of an internal-customer orientation. "You begin with executive commitment to the idea, but it quickly comes down to the skill and commitment of individual managers," Mr. Eggleston says. Ms. Bernard agrees: "We have concentrated on middle managers to bring about this change. Senior executives set the strategy and tone, but the deeds and actions of middle managers show employees that we truly intend to move in this direction."

Dr. Labovitz, professor of management at Boston University, is also president of Organizational Dynamics Inc., Burlington, Mass., a management consulting and training company.

Reprinted by ODI, 25 Mall Rd., Burlington, MA 01803, 617-272-8040, with permission of The Wall Street Journal. Copyright 1987. Dow Jones Co., Inc. All rights reserved.

THE WALL STREET JOURNAL.

MONDAY, OCTOBER 30, 1989

Speed on the Cycle Helps Companies Win the Race

Manager's Journal

by George H. Labovitz, Ph.D.

The rationale for responding to your customers' needs faster than the competition can is clear: Your company will benefit in terms of market share, customer satisfaction and profitability. In fact, managers today are probably more aware of speed as a competitive variable than ever before. However, for many, managing speed does not come naturally.

"Most of us grew up believing in the axioms 'Haste makes waste' and 'Don't cut corners,' ideas that seem to run counter to the concept of managing speed," says Dean Cassell, vice president for product integrity at Grumman Corp. "But in the real world, you learn that speed and quality are not a trade-off. Speed is a component of quality—one of the things we must deliver to satisfy customers."

Companies that actually market speed as part of their service train their managers to lead and participate in teams that increase speed and improve quality in everyday operations. Managers learn to spot opportunities to increase customer satisfaction through speed, and shift some responsibility for analyzing, improving and streamlining work processes from themselves to teams of employees.

One team at the Federal Express Ground Operations station in Natick, Mass., focused on a particularly time-sensitive operation: the morning package sort. Every morning, tractor-trailer trucks arrive at the Natick Ground Station from Boston's Logan Airport, carrying the day's package load. In peak periods that load may include 4,000 pieces. The packages must be sorted quickly and distributed to smaller vans for delivery, so couriers can be on the road by 8:35. No customer is present at the morning package sort, but the process is nevertheless critical to customer satisfaction.

"We're committed to deliver the customer's package by a stated time, usually 10:30," notes Glenn Mortimer, a Federal Express courier who led the Natick team. "The sooner our vans hit the road each morning, the easier it is for us to fulfill that obligation."

Following a problem-solving formula used by teams throughout Federal Express, members of the Natick team monitored their morning routine, carefully noting where and when the work group's resources were used effectively and where they were idle, waiting for others upstream in the process to send packages their way.

"We suspected there was downtime built into our process. But we didn't know just where it was until we completed our data gathering," Mr. Mortimer says. "We used the data to redesign our sorting system and put our resources where they could do the most good." The team even created a points system to identify those couriers and subgroups that were doing the most to reduce package-sort cycle time. Winners of the friendly competition earn a steak dinner out with their spouses.

"Monitoring shows that the Natick team's new system really does reduce cycle time for the morning package sort," reports James Barksdale, chief operating officer at Federal Express. "The vans leave at least 15 minutes earlier, on average, than they used to. And service levels have increased to the point where they're consistently above 99%."

A cross-functional team at Union Carbide's Tonawanda, N.Y., facility, which produces air-separation plants, followed a similar path to reduce manufacturing cycle time.

"The team included craftsmen from the shop floor as well as engineering, scheduling and purchasing personnel," reports Alan Westendorf, director of quality. "First, they produced a flowchart detailing the process by which an air-separation plant actually gets built. Then they identified snags in the process."

The Tonawanda team determined that holdups for inspections were the main problem and identified which kinds of delays involved critical inspections and which were less critical or could be handled by workers already on the line. The team then proposed modifications in their work process to management.

"The streamlined manufacturing process benefits our customers in at least two ways," Mr. Westendorf concludes. "First, we have better quality assurance than ever, because the people building the product have taken on more responsibility for the quality of their own work. Second, we

trimmed more than a month off the time required to deliver a finished product."

At Grumman's Aircraft Systems Division, a cross-functional team reduced the cycle time required to produce a new business proposal for an important government contract. The team was composed of representatives from engineering, manufacturing, corporate estimating, flight test, material, quality control, and other departments.

"We needed contributions from all these departments to generate the proposal," says Carl Anton, configuration-data manager for Grumman's A-6 combat aircraft program. "But instead of gathering their input piecemeal, we formed the team, which reached consensus on the proposal objectives and produced a statement of work to guide all the functions that were involved."

Armed with this shared understanding and requisite background information, each department developed its specialized contribution to the proposal, submitting data and cost estimates on a closely managed schedule. "We cleared up questions and inconsistencies very quickly, because the people who had the skills and perspective required to resolve them were part of the task team," Mr. Anton explains.

The team trimmed more than two months from the cycle time previously required to develop comparable proposals. "The team eliminated the crisis mentality that proposal deadlines can generate. The result was a more thoughtful, complete and competitive proposal," Mr. Anton concludes.

The successes achieved at Federal Express, Union Carbide and Grumman suggest that managing speed may be an underutilized source of competitive advantage. Managers in all three companies recognize speed as a component of quality and a key to customer satisfaction. They effectively lead team efforts to reduce cycle time. And they prepare all their people to increase the speed and improve the quality of their own work.

Dr. Labovitz, professor of management at Boston University, is also president of ODI, Burlington, Mass., a management consulting and training company.

QUALITY COSTS:
"The Good, The Bad and The Ugly"
By George H. Labovitz, Ph.D.
President, ODI
and Y.S. Chang, D.B.A.
Quality Counsel, ODI

Most executives are shocked when they first calculate the "cost of quality" — or the cost of "not doing the right things right" — in their own companies. And well they should be. Manufacturing operations commonly have a cost of quality equal to *one quarter of their total revenues*. In service companies, the figure is often *30% or more*.*

This means that in major corporations the costs associated with defects, missed schedules, budget overruns, complaint handling, overtime, billing errors and excessive turnover (to name just a few potential contributors to the cost of quality) can easily add up to *millions* of dollars each year.

Unfortunately, traditional cost cutting weapons (layoffs, inventory control, productivity improvement programs) only react to a few isolated costs after the fact. And they have no impact on most of the factors contributing to your cost of quality.

Yet in a few companies the cost of quality is much lower than the norm . . . perhaps one-half or even two-thirds below average. What are these companies doing differently?

Proactive Cost Management

To achieve lasting cost savings on a large scale, these companies plan and execute a truly *proactive* cost management strategy. And they

> **"The cost of quality is a great untapped reservoir of opportunity. Because every dollar saved from the cost of quality can be added directly to the bottom line."**

concentrate their efforts on preventing the *quality* problems at the root of most cost overruns.

Of course, this is no minor undertaking. It means building a "Total Quality" organization in which everyone who works in the company, in every department, from senior management through hourly employees, is dedicated to improving quality and meeting customer needs. The battle to reduce the cost of quality is a long one. In fact, it never ends. Because quality can always be improved further.

But a growing number of executives are willingly taking up the fight against quality costs. They recognize the cost of quality for what it is — a great untapped reservoir of opportunity. Every dollar saved from the cost of quality can be added directly to the bottom line.

In this article, we will focus on the beginning of *your* battle against quality costs by recalling the most basic rule of warfare, "Know thine enemy."

Understanding Quality Costs: "The Good, The Bad and The Ugly"

The first step to reducing your cost of quality is understanding that quality costs are *not* all created equal. Rather, they can be divided into three distinct categories:

1. Prevention Costs ("The Good")

2. Inspection/Correction Costs ("The Bad")

3. Field Failure Costs ("The Ugly")

1. Prevention Costs — "The Good" When is a cost "good"? When it is an *investment*.

Prevention Costs can be regarded as an investment because preventing (as opposed to correcting) quality problems makes your company much stronger over time.

---

*For an introduction to the "cost of quality," see our earlier management brief entitled, "Tough Questions Senior Managers Should Be Asking About Quality."

"Preventing quality problems makes your company much stronger over time."

Examples of Prevention Costs include your organization's investment in:

Quality Awareness programs to help managers, supervisors and employees understand the cost of quality, define their own roles in improving quality, and develop practical action plans for change.

Quality measurement and team problem-solving systems, through which *everyone* in your organization can identify and prevent potential mistakes before they happen.

Performance management systems to link hiring, training, appraisal, compensation and promotion to your quality improvement effort, so your people know that "quality counts."

These and other preventive measures are investments in your organization's future, as opposed to short-term "fixes" for problems that could easily arise again.

2. Inspection and Correction Costs — "The Bad"

Inspecting and checking other people's work is a role which virtually all managers and supervisors must fulfill each day. Yet in most cases, neither the inspector nor the inspected find this aspect of their job gratifying.

The time and money your organization spends on inspection — both through the formal Quality Control function and through management's informal checking of employees' work — is clearly "bad." It drains human and financial resources which could be used for more productive pursuits.

Worse yet, when inspection fulfills its mission and identifies errors or quality failures, the mistakes must still be *corrected.* And correction often causes expensive work stoppages or slowdowns that disrupt the routines and rhythms of your daily business.

Of course, you must have inspection and correction systems in your organization. But you should recognize that by themselves, they do nothing to reduce mistakes or improve quality. Even top Quality Control Departments — confronted by short-term "competing priorities" such as schedule and profits — may find themselves blocked from taking steps to measurably improve quality. They can only identify and correct quality failures as they happen and track costs for rework and scrap.

3. Field Failure Costs — "The Ugly"

Quality mistakes that turn up outside your organization, *after* your product or service is delivered to the customer, are ugly. Your company is cast in the worst possible light when it fails to meet your customer's valid requirements. (see box)

In hard dollar terms, field failure is by far the most costly quality problem. The cost of recalling and repairing defective products (or of "make good" on a service delivered unsatisfactorily) is extraordinarily high.

A good rule of thumb for comparing the relative costs of "The Good, The Bad and The Ugly" in your organization is the "1-10-100 Rule." For every dollar your company might spend on preventing a quality problem, it will spend ten to inspect and correct the mistake after it occurs. In the worst case, the quality failure goes unchecked or unnoticed until after your customer has taken delivery. To *fix* the problem at this stage, you'll probably pay about one hundred times what you could have paid to *prevent* it from happening at all.

---

*"Field Failure Costs" also occur *within* your company. Every large organization is comprised of a long chain of internal "customers" and "suppliers." Should the chain be broken at any point by failure to meet internal customers' own valid requirements, the quality of the product or service delivered to your external customers will almost certainly suffer.

Customer and Supplier Chain

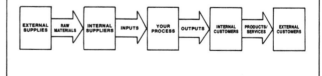

RELATIVE COSTS:
"THE GOOD, THE BAD AND THE UGLY"

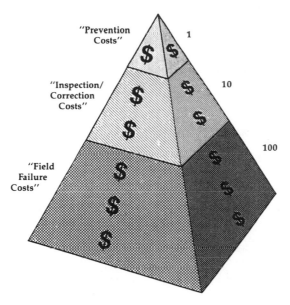

"Prevention Costs"

1

"Inspection/ Correction Costs"

10

100

"Field Failure Costs"

The "1 - 10 - 100 Rule"

competition take away business that would otherwise be yours.

The extent of the damage these "Ill Will Ambassadors" may actually inflict varies by the industry, company and individual involved. But the potential for harm posed by this "silent majority" should certainly keep your senior managers awake through the night.

So despite the expense of repairing field failures, each customer complaint should be seen as a "treasure"... a rare opportunity to prevent the creation of another "Ill Will Ambassador"... and a true beacon showing your company how and where to proceed in the continuous journey that is Total Quality Improvement.

CONCLUSION

By now, no doubt, our "prescription" for reducing your cost of quality is clear: *Invest* in prevention. Be sure everyone in your company understands the true cost of quality. And give your people the practical tools they need to make the "1-10-100 Rule" work *for*, not against, your company.

Many of the best companies are now implementing prevention processes that improve quality and reduce costs *simultaneously*. Their senior managers are attacking the cost of quality. And unlike their experience with other cost reduction approaches, they are finding that their people are behind them 100%. Because nearly everyone wants to be part of an organization that does things better than the competition.

As a leader, your choice is clear. You can continue to live with quality costs that may equal 25% or more of your total revenues. Or you can take decisive steps to master "The Good, The Bad and The Ugly," rally your organization around the issue of quality, improve your bottom line and ensure the future success of your company in an increasingly competitive world.

"Ill Will Ambassadors"

Still, you should count yourself lucky every time a customer gives you the opportunity to repair a defective product or service. Research indicates that 96% of your dissatisfied customers will never tell you about their quality complaint, and therefore never give you the chance to fix it.

Most dissatisfied customers will, however, take every opportunity to advise your other potential customers *not* to select your products or services. They will become "Ill Will Ambassadors" who undermine your company's reputation, reduce the effectiveness of your sales and marketing efforts and help your

---

"Dissatisfied customers become 'Ill Will Ambassadors' who undermine your company's reputation and help your competition take away business that would otherwise be yours."

The TQM Magazine (U.K.)

QUICK OFF THE MARK

JULIE SOQUET, DIRECTOR OF TRAINING, ODI EUROPE

Increased customer satisfaction is the driving force behind many organisations in the 1990s. ODI is helping companies achieve this goal through Quick-Start – a technique used to implement quickly and efficiently the management of both relationships and processes.

From Manchester to Melbourne to Minneapolis, businesses are changing – and so are the formulae for their success. Matrix management has turned hierarchy into history. And quality committed executives have turned organisations upside down by empowering employees to anticipate, meet, and exceed customer expectations.

At the heart of this dramatic change is an undying commitment to customer satisfaction and continuous quality improvement. This commitment is rooted in an understanding of the complex interactions required to satisfy the needs of internal and external customers, and the knowledge that customer satisfaction will be the driving competitive force of this decade. The bottom line is that in the global marketplace of the 1990s, the quality of products and services will depend on the extent to which people, at all organisational levels, manage work as a process.

The reality is that the success of these processes also depends on the relationships of the people who work in them. In essence, the continuous improvement of quality depends not only on effective process management, but on the interdependencies and relationships within an organisation. Both aspects of quality – process management and relationship management – are evident in the increasing use of the cross-functional team approach for improving quality.

ODI believes that establishing cross-functional teams of employees who work in the customer/supplier chain is critical to quality improvement. Our business, in part, is helping clients form cross-functional teams and then giving the teams methodologies that help them develop

solutions that increase customer satisfaction, decrease cycle time, and continuously improve quality.

Our approach focuses on relationship management as well as on process management – on guiding managers to reach beyond their personal piece of the organisation to understand the full range of functions that support key processes. There's no question that effective relationship management leads to successful process management. Only when managers, professionals, and non-managers learn to move comfortably across functional and interdepartmental barriers will they achieve continuous process improvement.

The challenge is to encourage people nurtured in hierarchical, self-contained organisations to look beyond their functional responsibilities to solve multi-functional process problems. The interdependencies that develop when teams focus on multi-functional process problems lead diverse groups to a common focus: customer satisfaction.

We encourage organisations to organise cross-functional quality improvement teams to tackle problems caused by the failure of multiple functions. Teams generally include a facilitator, a team leader (often the team member with the most at stake in the process – essentially the process 'owner') – and people representing the functions or organisations responsible for the specific process. The facilitator is frequently a consultant or manager not involved in the process. Along with the team leader, the facilitator creates an environment that enables individual team members to bring their expertise to the solution of multi-faceted, multi-functional problems. Additionally, the facilitator is an expert in problem-solving techniques and group dynamics, and focuses these integrated teams on developing integrated solutions. The overall value of this approach is that it focuses managers on improving the quality of the entire process, rather than on the improvement of 'independent' functions.

The first step in organising a cross-functional quality team is to identify the customer and the primary processes that serve the customer. Next, a commitment is negotiated, often directly with the chief executive officer, chief operating officer, or senior management team, to address problems associated with the process.

Once commitment is obtained – sometimes through a signed contract – a facilitator and team leader are appointed, team members identified, and the cross-functional team begins operation. Most teams meet once or twice a week for six to 12 months. And some cross-functional teams continue to meet regularly as a method of continuously overseeing their process.

The implementation of a cross-functional team approach often begins with an overview of quality improvement techniques and the problem-solving process. In fact, it's not unusual for companies to devote considerable time and resources to laying the groundwork for the process management approach to achieving quality. AT&T's Network Services Division, for example, is changing the organisation's approach to managing service after more than a century of hierarchical management. The Network Services Division – the core organisation that manages AT&T's Worldwide Intelligent Network – launched process

management through forums that communicated to managers the philosophy underlying this cross-functional approach; the organisation's model for changing roles, responsibilities, and relationships; and the organisational framework and tools for improving quality.

The division first identified four fundamental processes common to the services it provides AT&T's business units: service development, service management, service provisioning, and service maintenance. It then identified process owners (middle managers) and sub-process owners and charged them with accountability for the success of service enterprise. These owners are essentially the proprietors of mini-businesses comprised of cross-functional teams.

The composition of cross-functional teams depends on the direction of the quality planning effort. Some organisations form a senior management team, while others bring together a middle management team responsible for recommending process improvements to senior managers. Other organisations use cross-functional teams at the employee and supervisory level. Finally, some organisations choose an approach that involves all of the previous modes: a senior management team that defines the problem, and a middle management or supervisory and employee team that proposes and implements process solutions.

QUICK-START TEAMS

One of the most successful cross-functional approaches, Quick-Start, is adopted by organisations whose survival depends on their achieving immediate

success in solving critical quality problems. The Quick-Start process is designed specifically to provide swift process fixes and instant success stories.

The idea is to dedicate significant resources to 'jump start' quality improvement. Here, professional facilitators are a must. Unlike other approaches, the Quick-Start approach requires that team members meet several times a week for as long as two to three months to develop solutions. In most cases, the results are impressive – so impressive that Quick-Start initiatives often serve as role models for continuous quality improvement and the introduction and implementation of the total quality initiative in the rest of the organisation.

A critical aspect of the Quick-Start facilitator's role is supporting the team leader, who will serve as a catalyst for quality improvement. ODI's facilitators work directly with Quick-Start team leaders, coaching them in group dynamics and problem-solving methodologies. They help the leaders guide the team in changing processes and relationships.

The Quick-Start facilitator's role is especially important to the dynamics and the ultimate success of the team. Teams benefit from the professional's objectivity, his experience with quality initiatives in other organisations, and his ability to challenge norms and gain immediate authority.

An old-line American textile manufacturer, for example, credits the Quick-Start process with turning around a nearly bankrupt business. The firm faced increasingly fierce competition, rising customer dissatisfaction, and worsening financial conditions. Yet, senior managers knew that intensifying competition alone had not brought the business to the brink

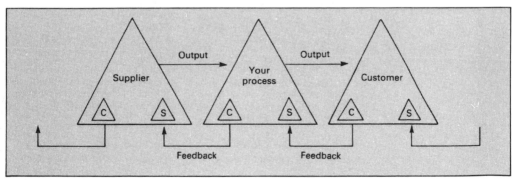

Customer/supplier chain.

of bankruptcy. Failure loomed because costs were high and quality low in virtually every part of the business.

In fact, deliveries lagged, defects were on the rise, inventory levels had soared, machinery frequently failed, and absenteeism had reached record levels. Most importantly, customer satisfaction had dropped to an all-time low. In short, every indicator crucial to the manufacturer's survival pointed to failure.

The firm responded with a Quick-Start process and total quality implementation. The manufacturer formed a cross-functional team of senior managers and their direct reports, and charged them with identifying performance indicators critical to quality and profitability. These managers organised teams of process owners (responsible for functions such as delivery and production) and asked them to find ways of dramatically reducing the cost of quality. The teams initiated changes that turned the business around in only one year.

Today, the company has achieved the following:

- On-time deliveries up by 22%.
- Product defects down by 33%.
- Inventory levels have fallen by 10%.
- Machinery downtime cut by 16%.
- Absenteeism decreased by 22%.

Competition is no less fierce. Yet, through Quick-Start, customer satisfaction is increasing dramatically.

Quick-Start also led to higher manufacturing efficiency and quality for a major aircraft manufacturer, troubled with excess amounts of scrap in aircraft component manufacturing and massive amounts of rework, delays, and shortages. A cross-functional team identified computer-generated operations sheets (guides used to translate engineering designs into assembled components) as the primary problem. The forms were poorly designed, and, as a result, the data was often incorrectly entered. And that was why the computer software erroneously identified essential parts. After studying the team's recommendations, the manufacturer rewrote the software. This action led to reductions in rework, delays, and inventory costs that now save half a million dollars annually.

Phillips Petroleum Company also credits the Quick-Start process with improvements in quality and profitability, with

Relationship management – influence through exchange

A critical component of cross-functional effectiveness is the team members' ability to manage relationships. To manage relationships effectively, team members must understand the 'world' in which other cross-functional team members 'live'. This understanding is central to the successful implementation of team recommendations, because such recommendations frequently require team members to influence others. And influence is optimised in the cross-functional team approach, where team members learn to create win-win situations in which all employees benefit from their interactions.

When cross-functional team members use organisational goals as a foundation, their mutual goals become apparent. By communicating goals, team members build an understanding of what is important for each person in the relationship and share 'relevant currency'. For example, daily data updates may be more important to me than the long-range plan. My 'currency' is timely and accurate data. Therefore, if you are trying to influence me to help you with a long-range planning project, your best approach would be to first tie it into my daily data needs.

In addition, it is helpful for team members to look at work styles. For example, some people prefer to begin work right away, while others start the day by chatting briefly about holidays or the latest football match. Some prefer to work independently, while others prefer group involvement. Understanding individual work styles will enhance the employees' ability to build strong cross-functional work relationships.

millions of dollars in annual savings in their costly and time-consuming maintenance turnaround work process. It was the company's practice to hire up to 1000 contract employees when it temporarily shut down one of the process units in a major refinery to perform routine equipment maintenance. The company challenged a cross-functional team of maintenance, engineering, and operations employees to evaluate the turnaround process and recommend ways to improve quality and reduce expenditure.

Among other findings, the study revealed that the firm could reclaim much of the maintenance work through improved planning and internal customer alignment, reducing the company's dependence on contractors. As already mentioned, the quality and productivity improvements represented millions in annual savings. Less quantifiable are the improvements in corporate culture: increased efficiency and greater interdepartmental cooperation.

Service businesses – and their customers – are also benefiting from the Quick-Start approach to improving quality. For example, a community hospital, located on the East Coast of the US, was experiencing consistent delays in scheduled surgery. In fact, 52% of the hospital's scheduled operations were, on average, nearly five hours late. The hospital organised a cross-functional team

consisting of the chief operating officer, the chief anaesthesiologist, the head of obstetrics and gynaecology, the director of radiology, the nursing director, two operating room nurses, the manager of patient transportation services, and a staff attorney.

The team found three primary causes for the delays:

- Physicians weren't ready at scheduled times.
- Patients were often delayed in testing and entry procedures prior to their operations.
- Staff people were often unavailable to move patients to operating rooms.

Through Quick-Start, the team developed and implemented recommendations that reduced the rate of delayed operations from the original 52% to 6%. The hospital decreased nursing overtime drastically, restructured preoperative procedures, and streamlined the flow of reports and patient data inside the hospital. As a result, patient satisfaction with the hospital's service is remarkably healthy.

Quick-Start is proving equally effective for global service businesses. American Express Bank, a major international bank that maintains a network of over 83 locations in 39 countries, adopted Quick-Start to solve problems associated with

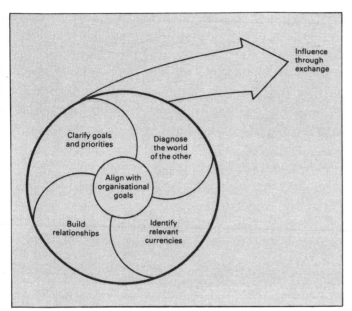

Relationship management.

the annual budgeting process. Early in 1990, American Express Bank formed a cross-functional team of managers representing key functions in the budgeting process: financial administration, network banking, strategic planning, and information systems. Led by a facilitator from the human resources department, within a four month time frame the 10-member team identified the major causes of the budgeting deadlock and developed 16 very diverse recommendations. Solutions included new approaches for submitting budgets; a total restructuring of the budget schedule; and streamlining the budget presentation process.

The success of this effort, as measured by the 1991 budget process, is difficult to quantify. They, nevertheless, achieved quality improvements in processes and relationships. The cross-functional team strengthened the link between the bank's strategic plan and profit targets – and it clearly reduced rework and overtime, and enhanced communications and working relationships. In fact, the team will continue to monitor the 1991 budget process, hoping to make further improvements to the 1992 budget process.

These results are not unusual. Although Quick-Start serves as an exceptionally effective quality 'booster', the methodology should be viewed as a beginning, not an end. Organisations committed to continuous quality improvement need to make a concerted effort to integrate the Quick-Start approach into their corporate culture. Neither Quick-Start, nor any other cross-functional team approach, can successfully stand alone. Experience confirms that the approach must be woven into the fabric of the organisation's overall quality improvement effort.

And, when that occurs, quality goes a long way towards achieving customer satisfaction – in the case of Federal Express, around the world. The objective of this international package carrier is to achieve 100% service levels on every customer transaction. That means over 1.3 million packages must move thousands of miles according to a precise timetable – every business day. More than 400 planes must take off and land on time, every time. Ground operations must operate like clockwork, and billing must be accurate.

Federal Express' approach to achieving 100% service excellence has been pure and simple: provide the structure, tools, and support FEDEX people need to improve their own work processes. The company's cross-functional team

approach is evidenced by a growing customer base – and the fact that the company recently became the first service business in the United States to earn the coveted Malcolm Baldrige National Quality Award.

But, Federal Express is not satisfied with the quality of its domestic operations. As the company's customers become increasingly global, Federal Express' goal is nothing less than marketplace leadership as the world's premier international full-service carrier. And, it is achieving this objective by putting cross-functional teams to work on key processes.

For example, since its merger with Tiger International, Inc (best known for its Flying Tiger air freight service), Federal Express is creating new cross-functional teams and integrating Flying Tiger employees into existing Federal Express teams. The overnight package carrier is using the quality improvement process to focus the energies of both organisations on a common cause: service perfection.

This challenge clearly demands both the process management and relationship management skills afforded by the cross-functional team approach to continuous quality improvement. Federal Express believes that effective teams not only cross functions, but also cross cultures and continents. ODI believes that Federal Express' philosophy is right on target. As businesses, large and small, become increasingly international, there's no question that achieving customer satisfaction will depend on cross-functional teams that span the globe. ☐

Julie Soquet is Director of Training, ODI Europe. She is an expert in domestic and international consulting, training, and programme design. She has developed and administered quality training programmes for clients in high-tech, health care, manufacturing, and government. Current and past clients include Alcoa, AT&T, Digital Equipment, Federal Express, General Motors, Hybritech, Moore Business Forms, Procter & Gamble, and the US Army.

At ODI she specialises in team building, problem-solving, quality training and implementation, and facilitator training design and delivery.

Ms Soquet brings to her consulting work a special understanding of the problems of cultures and groups within organisations. Before joining ODI, she was the director of training for an international training school. While there, she designed, administered, and published educational programmes for the United States Information Agency and worked on inter-cultural training for people transferring overseas.

The author has a BA from DePauw University, a MA in French from Middlebury College, and a MA in intercultural management from the School for International Training.

Communicating Total Quality Inside the Organization

The quality of communication often determines the ultimate success or failure of quality programs.

by Tom Varian

GOOD COMMUNICATION IS VITAL TO THE success of the total quality process. This is especially true of communication directed to audiences inside the organization. With proper execution, the right messages will contribute immeasurably to the success of the total quality process. Well-received communication will gain widespread commitment, rally the organization, and encourage action. Conversely, poorly managed communication might produce adverse effects.

Communication strategy is the least understood and most poorly managed aspect of many total quality management (TQM) implementations. Leaders of the total quality process often lack formal training or hands-on experience in communication management. Similarly, professional communicators frequently lack the in-depth understanding of TQM required to shape and execute an effective total quality communication plan.

A solution to this dilemma is to combine the knowledge and competency of total quality managers with that of communication professionals. Many organizations are doing this by forming communication task forces.

The following guidelines will help managers communicate total quality inside their organizations: making involvement the goal, providing a plan of action, developing a document with guidelines, providing an example of TQM in action, using existing internal communication channels, arming management to deliver the total quality message, reporting process achievements as well as results, and celebrating.

Making involvement the goal

If employees fail to become full and willing participants in the total quality process, TQM has failed. Therefore, involvement will be the meas-ure by which nearly everyone gauges the success of the total quality communication effort. Merely informing people about TQM is not enough; they must be motivated to take an active role.

Providing a plan of action

Senior managers are usually the first to grasp the strategic importance of TQM. But when they introduce it to the organization, they try to get the TQM message out as quickly and forcefully as possible. Unfortunately, this often leads to hasty, shallow, or overstated communication that threatens the long-term success of TQM.

This is most likely to occur in a large, complex organization, because senior management's initial announcement of the program is not often accompanied by immediate improvement opportunities for employees.

In the worst case, executives issue an urgent call to arms, but wait several months before offering managers and employees any practical opportunities for involvement in TQM (ad hoc or uncoordinated efforts are usually discouraged). All communication should be linked with specific options that managers and employees can act on. Similarly, reports about the first quality teams should include directions as to how and when others can form teams.

Linking TQM communications to specific suggested actions also helps measure the effectiveness of communication.

Developing a document with guidelines

Management should create a brief, easy-to-read document that introduces the quality process. This document should:
- introduce the TQM concept and explain how it is linked to business issues and other strategic initiatives.
- explain how TQM will be implemented.

- establish consistent terminology.
- establish clear expectations as to what will happen, when it will happen, and (in a general sense) how employees will be involved.

The tone of this document should be calm, serious, and optimistic. Everyone needs to understand that TQM is not an emergency, but a carefully considered plan that will ultimately benefit the organization and its customers.

Providing an example of TQM in action

Every large, complex organization is composed of numerous business groups or departments defined by function, geographic location, or hierarchy. Whether TQM is implemented through an organizationwide or unit-by-unit process, the largest and most influential business groups should be targeted for improvement first. This example will help other groups in the organization understand how TQM will affect their own work and goals.

Using existing internal communication channels

The goal is to make TQM an integral part of the organization's culture. Therefore, TQM messages should be communicated, whenever possible, through the organization's usual channels, as opposed to through new channels specifically created to communicate TQM information.

Common communication channels include internal newsletters, regular written or verbal reports from management, and orientation materials. TQM messages should be delivered through common channels to reinforce the idea that total quality is not an alien concept, but the foundation on which the organization operates.

Arming management to deliver the total quality message

Most organizations correctly look to management to deliver the quality message to business groups. Unfortunately, managers are often poorly equipped to fulfill this vital role. Many lack the background and perspective required to make the TQM message compelling and therefore might inform employees while failing to involve them.

Communication professionals can provide brief overhead, slide, or flip-chart presentations for managers and then train them to communicate effectively. Communications professionals can also suggest specific discussion points to help managers and their employees explore the total quality process as it applies to their own work.

Reporting process achievements as well as results

Skepticism often runs highest during the early stages of new programs, and support from results-oriented executives and managers is absolutely vital to getting the program off the ground. Yet, in the very early stages of TQM, tangible results are scarce. The first victories in building a TQM organization are almost always process achievements (e.g., formation of a quality council or the first quality teams) as opposed to measurable facts and figures.

Fortunately, process achievements can convey a strong sense of momentum and success when people throughout the organization are forming their own opinions about whether the TQM process is important. This makes it essential to publicize process achievements.

Publicizing the achievements of the first quality teams can provide an excellent opportunity to build a sense of accomplishment for all employees. Everyone in the organization should share in their trials and ultimate triumphs. To convey the information, one member of each team could keep a journal that would be published in serial form in an internal publication.

Celebrate

Celebrations can be the most powerful TQM communication tool. As the company completes each phase of its TQM implementation, it should find time to pause, rejoice, and recognize those who made each achievement possible.

Tom Varian is vice president of communications at ODI, Burlington, MA. He has a master's degree in history from Tufts University, Medford, MA.

Carlzon, Jan. *Moments of Truth*. New York: Harper & Row, 1989.

Crosby, Philip B. *Quality Is Free*. New York: McGraw-Hill, 1979.

Deming, W. Edwards. *Out of the Crisis*. Cambridge: Massachusetts Institute of Technology, Center for Advanced Engineering Study, 1986.

Feigenbaum, Armand V. *Total Quality Control*. New York: McGraw-Hill, 1983.

Goldratt, Eliyahu M. *The Goal*. Croton-on-Hudson, NY: North River Press, 1986.

Harrington, H. James. *The Improvement Process*. New York: McGraw-Hill, 1987.

Imai, Masaaki. *Kaizen: The Key to Japan's Competitive Success*. New York: Random House, 1986.

Ishikawa, Kaoru. *What Is Total Quality Control—the Japanese Way*. Englewood Cliffs, NJ: Prentice-Hall, 1985.

Jamieson, Archibald. *Introduction to Quality Control*. Englewood Cliffs, NJ: Prentice-Hall, 1981.

Juran, J. M. *Managerial Breakthrough*. New York: McGraw-Hill, 1964.

Pascale, Richard T. *Managing on the Edge*. New York: Simon & Schuster, 1990.

Peters, Thomas, J. *Thriving on Chaos: A Handbook for a Management Revolution*. New York: Alfred A. Knopf, 1987.

Townsend, Patrick L. *Commit to Quality*. New York: John Wiley & Sons, 1986.

Tzu, Sun. *The Art of War*. Boston: Shambhala Publications, 1988.

ODI is an international management consulting, training, and research company that specializes in total quality management (TQM). Founded in 1970 by George H. Labovitz, Ph.D., ODI is now among the largest TQM consulting and training firms with more than two hundred full-time employees and offices in seventeen U.S. cities and fifteen internationally. ODI headquarters is in Burlington, Massachusetts.

ODI serves Fortune 500 companies as well as medium-sized organizations in business, healthcare, and government. The company provides consulting services in TQM implementation planning and execution, and a full range of video-supported training programs, custom program development capabilities, and quality measurement software.

Air Force Logistics Command, American Express Bank, Arthur D. Little, AT&T, Baptist Memorial Health System, BellSouth Services, Chevron, Duke University Medical Center, the Environmental Protection Agency, Federal Express, General Electric, Grumman Corporation, Hybritech, the Joint Commission on Accreditation of Healthcare Organizations, L.L. Bean, Moore Business Forms, Nestlé Foods, Phillips Petroleum, Rockwell International, Shell, Texaco, Union Carbide, and UNUM Life Insurance are among the organizations served by ODI.

INDEX

"advance men," 142
advertising campaigns, 79–80
Affinity Diagram, 114, 115
Akers, John, 11
alignment, 6, 7, 51–55
American Express, 47
American Management Association, 50
Amoco Chemical Corporation, 60–61
  Quality Certificate of Accomplishment, 67
anti-trust laws, 73
authority
  See Employee(s): empowerment of

"backwardation," 84, 86–87
Baltimore Gas & Electric, 62
benchmarking, 117–18, 119
Brain Dominance Model, 96–98
Breakthrough Leadership, 110–44, 147
  "advance men" in, 142
  benchmarking in, 117–18, 19
  Cascading Goals in, 120–23, 148
  consensus cultivation in, 113–17, 141, 144
  customer-focused, 115, 117, 118, 128, 133, 135, 142, 144, 148, 149–51
  deployment in, 111, 118–33, 142, 143, 144
  objectives in, 112–13, 114, 118, 120–21, 127, 132–33, 142
  planning in, 111, 112–16, 118, 121, 142–43, 144
  review in, 111, 121–24, 135–42, 143, 144
Brigman, Brenda, 130–31
Buzzell, Robert D. and Gale, Bradley T., *PIMS Principles: Linking Strategy to Performance, The*, 48–49

Cahill, John, 35–37, 41
Cascading Goals, 120–23, 148
Catchball, 114–15, 116, 148
Celanese Corporation, 61
CEO role, 12, 105–6, 107, 108, 133–35
  See also Leadership; individual CEOs
Chang, Yu Sang, 2, 3, 4, 8, 9, 29–30
change, 17, 46, 63, 67–68, 81, 117
charisma, 134, 135
Chessie System, 59
  See also CSX Transportation
"chimneys," 16, 125
  See also Management hierarchies
Chrysler Corporation Research and Development Center, 125
  "tiger team" achievements, 125
competitive advantage, 6, 7–8, 21, 42, 61, 69, 73, 80, 89, 90, 111, 117
  quality as, 7–8, 9, 33, 47–68
competitive challenges, 8, 9–10, 27
consensus cultivation, 113–17, 141, 144
Corning, Inc.:
  CEO leadership role, 135
corporate culture
  See Organizational culture
cost-benefit analysis, 22
cost control and reduction, 27, 37, 59, 61, 64, 77, 80, 84, 87, 94, 96, 99, 103, 105, 123
credit reports, 66
crisis management and prevention, 13, 14, 16, 17, 23–25, 26
Crosby, Philip, 62, 191
  Quality Is Free, 4–5, 191
cross-functional teams, 16

See also "Tiger teams"
CSX Transportation, 59–67
  awards won, 66–67
  customer-supplier relationships, 60–61, 63, 65–67, 72
  deregulation impact, 59–60, 61
  downsizing, 60
  employee injuries, 66, 67
  "Quality Cascade" performance of, 60–63
  stock price performance of, 67
  TQM at, 64–65
  union role at, 64
  Voice of the Customer at, 63, 65–66
cultural diversity, 78–79
customer(s), 7
  ultimate, 72, 74–75, 78, 79, 83, 84, 85, 87, 89
customer focus, 89–90, 115, 117, 118, 128, 133, 135, 142, 144, 148, 149–51
customer loyalty
  See Customer-supplier relationships
customer requirements, 6, 9, 13, 15, 22–23, 61, 75, 101, 110, 111, 128–29, 138
  See also Voice of the Customer
customer satisfaction, 1, 8, 9, 11, 14, 15, 16, 17, 41, 45, 60, 65–66, 69–70, 74, 92, 93–94, 95–96, 98, 105, 110, 111, 119, 123, 124, 128, 147, 150, 152, 156–57
  and repeat business, 50, 156–57
  See also Delight
customer-supplier relationship, 7, 8, 9, 13, 14, 17, 21, 49–50, 71–90, 117, 120–21, 148–49, 150, 151, 154–56
  accommodation in, 71–72
  partnerships, 72–90
cycle time, 26, 75–77, 103, 120

Daewoo Corporation, 142
data gathering, 7, 13, 14, 15–16, 17, 18, 23, 31, 38–39, 65–66, 70, 102, 126, 127–28, 138, 151
delight, as goal, 11, 13, 18, 53, 54, 55, 61, 111, 120, 147, 148, 150, 151
Deming, W. Edwards, 4, 5
Deming Prize, 1, 99, 171, 172–73
deregulation, 59–60, 61
discounting, 74–75
Dow Chemical, 61–62
downsizing, 60, 64, 92
downtime, 112
duPont (E. I.) Outstanding Carrier award, 67

Economist, The, 11, 12
Eli Lilly & Company, 103
employee(s):
  attitude of, 2, 10, 13, 21, 23, 35, 41, 50, 63, 64–65, 91–92, 123, 124, 131–32, 149, 150
  as customers, 30, 62, 96
  empowerment of, 13, 14–15, 16, 19, 23, 34, 35, 36, 37, 38–39, 40, 46, 92–93, 94, 100, 101, 106, 111, 118, 119, 133, 137, 138, 143, 144, 147, 149, 150, 152, 153
  grievances of, 94–95
  injuries of, 66, 67, 94, 126
  participation of, 1, 2, 4, 14–15, 16, 19, 23, 34, 35, 36, 37, 38–39, 40, 46

entrepreneurism, entrepreneurial roots, 27, 30–32, 37, 40, 41, 46
European shipping businesses, 78–79
Evans, Rob, 81
executive review, 135–42, 143, 144, 148

Federal Express:
  corporate philosophy, 34, 35
  cultural diversity management by, 78–79
  customer expectations, 128–29
  data-gathering mechanisms, 7, 82
  management goals, 34–35, 36, 40, 81–82, 128
  partnering principles used by, 78–79, 81–82
  People-Service-Profit, 34, 35
  root-cause teams, 130–32
  Service Assurance Manager (SAM) role, 131–32
  Service Quality Indicator (SQI), 7, 128–32
  Survey-Feedback-Action, 7, 37, 38–39, 40, 41
  TQM program, 6–7, 41
  ultimate customers of, 81, 82
  Voice of the Customer, 32–33, 34, 40
  Voice of the Employee, 35–40, 41, 105–6
  Voice of the Process, 40, 41–45
feedback, 31, 38–39, 137, 143, 149, 151, 153
  See also Performance measurement
Feigenbaum, Arnold V., 4, 191
  Total Quality Control, 99, 191
Fiore, Tony, 36
Fletcher, Joe, 64
Florida Power & Light, TQM program, 3–4
flowcharting, 130
focus groups, 70
  See also Data gathering
Ford Motor Company, 61–62
Fortune, 133–34
Fortune 500 companies, 2
  See also individual companies
French shipping businesses, 78–79

Gage, Tim, 155, 156, 157
Gale, Bradley T., 48–49
Galvin, Bob, 101–2, 106
General Motors, 41
Gingrich, Newt, 1
goals
  See Objectives; Performance measurement
Goldratt, Eliyahu M., *Goal, The,* 99, 191
Grimm, Don, 103-5, 106
Grumman Corporation:
  cycle time reduction, 103
  Long-Life Vehicle (LLV) division, 154–57
  Performance Award bonuses, 155–56
  process-improvement method, 103
  Quick-Start team savings, 103
  TQM program, 154–57
  Voice of the Customer, 155, 156–57
  Voice of the Employee, 156

Hantz, Ed, 154
hard vs. soft skills, 8–9
Harvard University, 48
Hawk, Dale, 58–60, 61, 62, 63, 64–66
Herrmann, Ned, 96, 97
Herrmann Brain Dominance Model, 96–97, 98
Hewlett, Bill, 30

Hewlett-Packard
  middle-management role, 114
Hewlett-Packard Medical Products Division,
  29–30
  customer-supplier relationships, 29–30, 62
hoshin kanri 110–11
  See also Breakthrough Leadership
Houghton, Jamie, 134–35
Hybritech, 103, 105
  profitability improvements, 105
  TQM program, 105
  Voice of the Customer, 105

Iacocca, Lee, 125, 126
Imai, Masaaki, *Kaizen: The Key to Japan's Compet-
  itive Success,* 99, 191
International Business Machines (IBM):
  attitude at, 2
  customer-supplier relationships, 11, 61–62
  quality control techniques, 2
  TQM programs, 1–2
International Customer Service Association ICSA
  Award of Excellence, 67
inventory control, 77, 84, 87, 88, 103, 119, 120
invoicing, 66, 76–77, 84, 87, 119, 129
Ishikawa, Kaoru, 4, 137–38
Italian shipping businesses, 78–79

Jackson, Darryl, 42–45
James River Corporation Gold Key Service
  Award, 67
Japan:
  "advance men" in, 142
  consensus cultivation in, 113–14
  customer-supplier relationships, 29–30, 45,
    101–2
  textile industry in, 42–43
  "tiger team" in, 126
  TQM in, 2, 3, 4
  work process management, 42–43
  See also Breakthrough Leadership; individual
    leaders and companies
Juran, Joseph, 4
just-in-time systems, 77, 84, 87

Kansai Electric Company, 1–2
  TQM at, 2
Korea, "advance men" in, 142

Labovitz, George H., 2–3, 9
Laco, Tom, 5, 6, 7
leadership, 81–82
  accountability of, 93, 131
  compassion in, 106–7
  by example, 8, 9, 15, 24, 27, 34, 150
  as "magic ingredient," 95, 98–99, 110, 143–44
  passion in, 106, 157
  in TQM companies, 96–108, 109–10, 150
  visits by, 15–16, 61–62, 99, 105, 117, 133–42,
    144
  world-class, 8, 9–10, 18, 21, 22, 23, 27, 33,
    43–44, 45–46, 67–68, 89, 92–93, 95, 110,
    148, 158
  See also Breakthrough Leadership

Lee, Byung Chull, 2
L.L. Bean:
  Voice of the Customer, 32, 33
  Voice of the Process, 33–34
Loughead, Bob, 106
LTV Steel Outstanding Supplier Award, 66

McDonald, Marshall, 3
Malcolm Baldrige National Quality Award, 41,
  45, 46n, 50, 99, 114
management:
  authoritarian vs. participatory, 91–92, 93, 101,
    106, 133
  middle, 107–8, 109, 110, 114, 137
  See also Leadership
Management by Objectives, 3, 95
management culture
  See Organizational culture
management hierarchies, 14, 32–33, 37, 40, 41,
  75, 87, 108, 114–15, 125, 136
management information systems, 73
management roles and priorities, 2, 4, 5, 6, 14,
  21–22, 34–36, 37, 40, 64–65, 88
  quality as, 4–5, 63–64
management systems, 62, 73
management training programs, 2–3, 8–9, 11,
  15, 64–65, 94, 137
Milliken, Roger, 42–44, 45, 106
Milliken & Company, 42–45
  Voice of the Customer, 45
  Voice of the Employee, 45
  Voice of the Process, 44–45
Minnesota Mining & Manufacturing (3M), 62
mission, communication of, 111, 135
MIS systems, 73
Monsanto Chemical Company, 61
Moore Corporation
  Quality Site Review (QSR), 139–41
Motorola, Inc.:
  TQM programs, 101–2
  Voice of the Customer, 101–2
M.S. Carriers, 42

NEC Corporation, 29
"not invented here" syndrome, 133

objectives
  achievement of, 2, 7, 112–13, 114, 118,
    120–21, 127, 132–33, 142
ODI
  See Organizational Dynamics, Inc.
Oil, Chemical, and Atomic Workers Union,
  91–93
Oliver, Tom, 32–33, 35
operating efficiency, 21, 44
Opportunity Gap, 52–53, 54–55, 56, 90
organizational autonomy, 14
organizational culture, 5, 6, 27, 40, 62–63, 89
Organizational Dynamics, Inc. (ODI), 2–3, 5,
  6–7, 9, 93, 103, 106
  "backwardation" at, 84, 86–87
organizational mass, 41
organizational strengths, 13, 14, 15, 18
organizational weaknesses, 13, 14, 15, 18

packaging, 77–78
Pascale, Richard T., *Managing on the Edge,* 99, 191
Peixotto, Bob, 32
performance measurement, 7, 65–66, 67, 88, 102, 121–24
  employee reviews, 152–53
  executive reviews, 135–42, 143, 144, 148
Personal Quality Audit, 56–59, 101
Peters, Tom, *Thriving on Chaos,* 99
PIMS
  See Profit Impact of Market Strategy (PIMS) project
PRIDE checklist, 85
  See also Customer(s): ultimate
priorities, 15, 65–66, 100, 112, 114–15
problem-solving, 17, 31, 96, 125
  See also Crisis management and prevention; Voice of the Process
process improvement, 17, 23, 38, 102, 103, 137–38, 142
  See also Voice of the Process
process management team
  See "Tiger teams"
Procter & Gamble:
  advertising campaigns, 79–80
  customer-supplier relationships, 7, 72, 74–78, 79–80, 82–84, 88
  inertia at, 5
  just-in-time shipping system, 77, 84, 87
  organizational culture, 5, 6
  package design, 77–78
  Preferred Quality Supplier Award, 67
  statistical process control training, 5
  TQM program, 5–6, 51, 72
  ultimate customers of, 74–75, 77–78, 79–80, 82–83, 88
product development, 77–78, 80
productivity, 27, 92, 131–32
profitability, 34, 48, 49, 51, 55, 56, 67, 92, 95, 96, 105, 123
Profit Impact of Market Strategy (PIMS) project, 48–50

quality, quality improvement, 8, 11, 15, 16, 33, 44, 98, 132–33, 151, 154–56
  as competitive advantage, 7–8, 9, 33, 47–68, 158
  "conformance," 49
  continuous nature of, 62
  corporate failure to achieve, 11–12
  cost-effectiveness of, 4–5
  as "hot issue," 5
  individual contribution to, 56–59
  as management problem, 62
  "perceived," 48–50
  profitability of, 48, 67
quality action teams, 94, 100, 102–3, 105
  See also "Tiger teams"
"Quality Cascade," 60–63
quality circles, 4
quality control, quality-control techniques, 2, 5, 84, 87
Quality Digest, 12
Quality Function Deployment, 117
quality goals:
  defensive, 54, 56
  offensive, 55, 56
quality problems, 25, 52
  See also specific problems
quality teams, 12, 15
  See also "Tiger teams"
quality tools, as concepts, 5–6

Railo, Willi, 107
recognition
  See Rewards and recognition
  return on investment, 48, 81
  See also Profitability
rewards and recognition, 149, 150, 151–56
rework, 26, 59, 62, 66, 80, 93–94, 103, 120, 155, 156
Rework Gap, 52, 54, 56, 95
Robinson, Jim, 47
Rosansky, Victor I., 3, 7, 74–75, 78, 79
Ross, Rosita, 132

Samsung Group, 2
Saudi Refining, Inc., 95
Seaboard Coast Line, 59
  See also CSX Transportation
service calls, 120
short-term vs. long-term thinking and planning, 13, 14, 15, 27, 71–72, 102
Smith, Fred, 6, 8, 34–35, 36, 45, 105–6
Snow, John, 61–62, 63
Sparks, Jerry, 91–93, 95, 108
SPC
  See Statistical process control
SPI
  See Strategic Planning Institute
Star Enterprise, 95
statistical process control, 5
Strategic Planning Institute (SPI), 48–50
suggestion systems, 16, 156
Sun Tzu, *Art of War, The,* 99
surveys, 70
  See also Data gathering

Tapping the Network Journal, 11
task force
  See "Tiger teams"
team problem-solving, 4, 102
  See also "Tiger teams"
Technical Assistance Research Programs, 50
technology, 53
Texaco, Inc., Port Arthur refinery, 91–95, 99–100
  customer-supplier relationships, 92, 93–94
  employee grievances, 94–95
  employee injuries, 94
  management role, 108
  quality action teams, 94, 100
  union role, 91–95, 100
  Voice of the Customer, 93–94, 100
  Voice of the Employee, 93, 100
Texaco Refining and Marketing, Inc., 95
3M, 62
"tiger teams," 125–28, 130–32, 133
Total Quality Management (TQM), 1, 3, 40
  Active stage, 12, 13, 15–17
  application of, 5
  Awakening stage, 12, 13, 14

Total Quality Management *(cont.)*
  Breakthrough stage, 12, 13, 17
  commitment to, 103–8
  failure of, 11–12
  means and ends of, 18–19
  road map needed, 12, 18–19
  value-driven nature of, 95–96, 98, 99
  World-Class stage, 12, 13, 18
  See also individual leaders and companies
Townsend, Lee, 92–94, 95, 99–100, 106, 108
Toyota Motor Corporation, 29
Trade-offs, 21–27
training and development, 148, 149, 150
"turfism," 13, 14, 17, 18

Union Carbide Rail Carrier of the Year award, 67
unions, 91–95, 100
U.S. General Accounting Office, 50
U.S. Office of Consumer Affairs, 50
U.S. Postal Service, 155, 156–57
  Supplier Quality Award, 157
United Technologies Pratt & Whitney division,
    performance appraisal system, 152–53

value:
  added, 15, 17
  unexpected, 9, 13, 53, 54
  See also Delight
values
  communication of, 8, 106, 111
Varian Associates, Inc., Cascading Goal approach,
    120–21
vision, communication of, 100, 101
Voice of the Customer, 6, 22, 23, 25–26, 29–34, 40,
    51–52, 54, 55, 63, 94, 115, 117, 118, 147, 158

Voice of the Employee, 6, 22–23, 34–41, 51–52,
    54, 55, 63, 93, 110, 118, 147, 158
Voice of the Process, 6, 23, 33–34, 40, 41–45,
    51–52, 54, 55, 110, 118, 158
Voltaire, François Marie Arouet, 48

Wall Street Journal, 11
Wal-Mart Stores:
  CEO leadership role, 133–34
  customer-supplier relationships, 7, 72, 74–78,
    82–84, 88
  cycle time improvement, 76, 84
  just-in-time inventory system, 77, 84, 88
  process efficiency improvement, 76, 87, 88
  TQM program, 72
  ultimate customers of, 74–75, 77–78, 82–83,
    88
Walton, Sam, 7, 76, 87, 89, 133–34, 135
Weirton Steel, 106
West, John, 128–29
workflows, work processes, 23, 24–25, 38, 42,
    43–45, 51, 52, 62, 65–66, 72–73, 75–77, 81,
    83, 87, 88, 93–94, 100, 101, 117–19, 120,
    125, 126, 128, 130–31
  continuous improvement as goal in, 132–33

Xerox Corporation:
  Business Process List, 119–20
  goal documentation and measurement,
    121–24

zero defects, 1, 3, 8, 95, 101
zero downtime, 112
Zytech, Inc., 114